I0529780

Write and Publish Your First Book

A Step-By-Step Blueprint to Write, Self-Publish and Market Your Fiction or Non-Fiction Book

Lorna Faith

Book Reviews

For all those who are trying to find a way to reach their writing dreams ~ this one's for you.

Introduction

Why I Wrote This Book

Your work - what you create - tells your story.

It lays bare your hopes, your dreams and speaks about what matters most to you. It shows people what you really think of the world around you.

Your voice needs to be heard.

However, you must be willing to be brave. You are the only one who can choose to let your original self - your ideas and life - be heard.

You're the only one who can uncover, grow and ultimately be courageous enough to share your unique thoughts and ideas with others.

I'm passionate about helping people uncover and begin to use their authentic voice. For too many years, I hid in my safe little world.

And because of different moments of pain and trauma from my childhood, I lost what it was like to be me for a while. I desperately wanted to uncover my authentic voice, but didn't know how to find it again.

I was scared this farm-girl turned homeschooling mom, didn't have what it took to step out to reach her dreams of writing page-turning stories.

I really thought about writing for a long time - for over twenty years - before I even put pen to paper. I stopped writing stories in Elementary School after a teacher I admired told me my writing was like *chicken scratchings*. Being a farm-girl, I knew what that meant.

I was devastated.

I didn't pick up a pen to write my story again for over twenty years. It was only as I started home-schooling my own four children about how to write stories that suddenly the dream to write came back stronger than ever.

I didn't know if I could do it. I put it off, but my dream wouldn't let go of me.

So, I finally decided that at the very least *I could try and learn to write a story.*

I started.

I made the effort to learn a little bit everyday. I poured hundreds of hours into reading books, blogposts and listening to podcasts so that I could lear n what it really took to write, self-publish and market a book. From the beginning, as I learned to write and up to the point where I was ready to self-publish the book, it took me eight years.

When I got to the editing stage of the book, I had the help of a professional editor. But it took me six months longer than I thought it would to get the book edited and out into the world.

It was such a steep learning curve, there were many days I wasn't sure if publishing the book would ever happen. But it did. I finally got my first historical romance written and self-published. I was thrilled.

Why did it take me so long?

The reason is simple. I thought I needed to wait to be picked. In my mind, I needed the approval of a gatekeeper in the publishing world - an agent or a publisher - to tell me I was a writer. I was afraid of being rejected. I'd experienced that feeling too many times before and didn't like it.

I didn't believe I was good enough to write my own stories, without messing it up completely. I thought if I tried to write my own book, that I would ruin the story and I might even wreck any chances I had to get any future books out there.

This was a new kind of learning that somehow seemed more difficult than even the hard physical labor that farm work asked of me.

I was intimidated, scared of rejection and worried that somehow I wouldn't be able to take the steps needed to get closer my writing dream.

Yet, there were a couple of things I had going for me.

I had a strong desire to learn and the grit to keep after it day after day.

But, here's the thing. I never forgot the struggle I went through to learn what I needed to, in order to write, edit, self-publish and then try to market my first book.

It was such a huge struggle for me and such a steep learning curve that I've made it my goal to do what I can to help first-time writers. I want to help make the process so much easier for new writers who are thinking about writing and self-publishing their first book.

A quick update: Since first publishing this book seven years ago in 2015, I have written and self-published more books under my Lorna Faith author name and another eight sweet romances under a pen name. As of this writing, I am happily earning four figures a month with my pen name fiction books alone.

If I can do this, you can too!

In fact, that's the reason for writing this book. I wanted to give you a layout of what it takes to go from hardly knowing a thing—like where I was when I started—to having the details you need to self-publish your book and upload it up to digital retail stores like *Amazon, Kobo, Apple, Google Play Books, Nook and others.* I've also been learning how to setup a digital retail store on my author website.

I'm excited for you as a new writer, I really am. The writing and digital publishing world has never looked brighter than it is right now.

Introduction

There are many successful indie authors who are *mid list* authors who are making a living with their writing. If your goal is to make a living with your writing, you can do that too.

The hardest part on this journey, is to be focused to write everyday, to set your goals and learn all you can along the way from other authors. However, I believe you can do this.

Writing is on the *I-really-want-to-do-this* list for 81% of people, but most will never do it. They won't even start. I hope you won't be one of those that gave up before they begin. I really hope you give yourself the chance to fulfill your writing dream.

I want to encourage you to begin today. Get five hundred words written before you go to sleep tonight. You'll be so happy you did.

It's a great place to start, and one that you can repeat tomorrow. Keep writing and get that first draft done as quickly as possible.

I hope you have fun in this process and that your books will sell like crazy! I'd love to hear about your story and about your writing journey.

Please do stop by www.createastoryyoulove.com and let us get to know each other.

If you're excited to learn how to get your story out into the world, please read on...

Please Note: Some of the website links I mention within this book are affiliate links to products and services that I recommend and use personally. This means that I receive a small percentage of sales with no extra cost to you and you may receive a discount for using my links. I only recommend services I believe in and use and are great for authors!

Chapter One

W hy You should Write Your Book Now

If you've been waiting and dreaming of the perfect time to write, I want to encourage you to stop waiting.

Now is the best time to write and self-publish your book.

Maybe you've heard the myth out there that says *books are dead* and that no one reads them anymore.

It seems like almost everyone online is talking about other ways of consuming content like podcasts, audio and video and how they are the next best thing since sliced bread.

I love podcasts, audio and video and I've learned a lot from each of those mediums, but to think that they could replace books? That's crazy talk! It's not going to happen.

Books have been around for hundreds of years and they aren't going away any time soon.

In fact with the introduction of digital books, being a writer is more exciting than ever.

If you think about it, it seems like everywhere you look people have a mobile device of some kind. With iPad, Android and Kindle devices outselling computers right now, it's not surprising that we see companies like Google, Apple, and Amazon making the most of these mobile devices by selling music, apps, movies and ebooks.

These companies and their products seem to follow you everywhere you go. Not only do these companies have unlimited access to you, but also to people who buy your books. People from all over the world in almost every country and language have access to ebooks.

When you publish your ebook on Amazon, they'll pay you 70% of sales while promoting your work to all these millions of people.

And all it takes is one click for people to buy and have your ebook on their digital device, which you have access to for free.

So when you blend unlimited free distribution, endless shelf space and mix it with super easy access for readers, the possibilities of reaching a lot of readers for your books is incredible.

The best part is that for you as an author this is

passive income and your book grows your list of readers and positions you as an authority in your niche.

How exciting is that?

These are all great reasons to write your book now.

Create the Space You Need to Write

Maybe you don't think that you could write a book. Perhaps you were told, somewhere in your past, that your writing is just not good enough. Or maybe you think writing a book seems like too big of a task.

If that's you, I want to encourage you not to give up. Push past your fears. I believe you can do it, because those are the same doubts and fears that I faced when I began writing my first fiction book.

Here's something I learned during those years that I was dabbling with writing and hesitating because of fear and doubt.

There's never going to be a perfect moment.

Life is still going to happen all around you. I you have children, your kids will need your help. If you have a day job, that will still happen. Your husband or wife will still need your attention. Life will go on.

However, if your goal is to get a book written this year - which is very doable by the way - then you'll need to take the first step to make it happen.

I discovered that the best way to silence fear and doubt is to move forward anyway.

I realized that I'd rather try and fail a bunch of

times, then sit back and wonder what might have been. Wouldn't you?

Of course, this will mean some of those things that are taking up extra time in your life will need to be sacrificed in order to get your book finished and self-published.

Maybe you'll need to limit your TV time, or curb the number of visits or parties with friends and other things that are stealing what little free time you have. At least that's what I needed to do, to get my book written and self-published.

I had to put boundaries on my time when I started writing. I had to tell my teenagers that, when the door is closed to my room, I'm writing. So, unless it's something really important, please don't disturb me.

I also chose to only watch a little TV each week and the rest of the time I would write in one of my projects I had on the go.

Sometimes it's more than lack of time that holds us back from writing those words we long to write. I know that was how it was for me. I hid my dream in the shadows for so many years because I was *afraid to go there.*

For far too long I believed the lie that there was going to be a perfect moment to write. Or worse, I thought I had to be picked. I believed that because I had never written a book before, that I wasn't good enough. That I would completely fail and no one would be interested in anything I had to write.

Turns out I was wrong. There were quite a few people who liked what I wrote, even though I hadn't been picked by an agent or publishing house. That was when I started to think that maybe I could be a writer. Even though I'm still publishing books, with lingering doubts and fear, I don't let the fear immobilize me anymore.

So how did I get from a place where I held back in fear, to the point where I could write and self-publish books? That's what I want to share with you.

Read on, because I want to help you move beyond fear and procrastination, to unlock your creativity, uncover your natural writing voice and self-publish your book.

Unlock Your Authentic Voice

There has been a lot of attention given to the idea of finding your voice as a writer. I really do believe that everyone has their own unique voice.

Our voice is something we need to uncover as writers. It's really that simple.

I used to think of authors as being too far above me and I thought of writing in much the same way. I thought I needed to find those difficult, fifty cent words and that would be the game-changer for me.

I was convinced that was how I would discover my writing voice. But that way of thinking - believing that writing was difficult and far above me - was actually the biggest roadblock to uncovering my real voice.

You see, for each of us as writers, the moment we think of writing as something too unreachable, or we start believing we need to "cook up" something - *a voice* - in order to be able write, our natural voice is blocked.

When we believe that, writing becomes unattainable and an impossible art rather than something we were born to do.

It's important to simply begin. Start where you are. Don't worry about finding your voice. Instead just allow yourself to step fully into what you want to say and in that way you will intuitively show up as the real, authentic you on the page.

In some ways, writing reminds me of singing. You see, I spent twenty years being trained as a singer.

When my singing teacher wanted to open up and unlock my authentic voice, the first step was to develop proper breathing. To take deep breaths with the diaphragm - from the gut - and learn to do it regularly.

Our writing voice is much the same. To open up our writing voice, the best way to unlock our authentic self is to write from the gut, regularly and repetitively.

What has helped me to unlock my creativity, is to write what Julia Cameron in her book *The Artist's Way*, calls Morning Pages. It takes me about thirty minutes to write three pages of whatever comes into my mind.

Writing morning pages is a little like doing vocal scales. It takes you up and down your feelings of whatever you're going through that day. Writing these pages each day lays the foundation of writing from the gut.

As with singing, this is a writer's breathing exercises. From this core, everything you write rests on this.

Doing these morning pages and writing them freely, without editing or self-censoring, is not a waste of time.

In fact it will help you unlock your creativity and your voice so that you can write your novel and your other books freely and easily.

When you learn to sing, you start by learning vowels and opening your mouth to begin to get a good tone. This is the basis for developing a beautiful singing voice.

It's similar with writing. When you write from your gut - your truest self - you will unlock and continue to develop a writing voice that is full and beautiful no matter what kind of books you write.

Writing from the gut - digging down into the deep well of your experiences and listening to how you feel - produces a full body of work.

Writing from our gut instead of our head will train us to gain access to the same resonance a singer does when the breath comes from deep within the diaphragm rather than from the chest voice.

When you are writing in your natural, authentic voice, you are writing by listening to how you feel, rather than by overthinking about how you feel and the right words to use.

This is how you bypass your self-editor. Some days it's easier to get around the censor than other days. Some days it seems to be especially hard on you and other days it's just annoying.

The trick is to keep writing despite what the censor has to say. Morning Pages helps writers to keep writing despite that inner editor.

It's a beautiful thing to begin to listen to yourself and to what the deepest part of you is saying. This is the kind of writing you do when you are writing to someone who gets you. It's the writing you do when you feel safe.

More often than not, this is also your most simple, yet honest and real writing you do. It comes when you're writing for your ideal reader, instead of writing for *everyone*. Your ideal reader will get you and everything you say. It's this reader that makes you feel safe.

It's when you are listening to what wants to come out that you will discover your true voice.

As you surrender your ideas of how your words should look and sound, and let the art come out how it wants to, this is honest and raw writing that is not contrived. This is writing from the gut and is the truest version of you.

As you continue to practice writing everyday, these daily exercises will give you the skills and confidence to bring out the voice that wants to move through you.

At the end of the day, your authentic voice is how you express your burning "why." You want to speak from a deep understanding of what you care about and find a way to bring the one-of-a-kind value that only you can bring.

Something to try...

An exercise that will help you begin to uncover your authentic voice is to begin to write small scenes you remember from your past that have an emotional stake for you. It's like writing little stories from your life.

For example, you could write about your family's secrets, a favorite relative, a near death experience, your closest friend or your happiest memory.

Writing these short scenes, focused on one experience, helps you speak from an emotional truth which in turn unlocks your authentic voice.

Try writing these scenes using the voice from your childhood. Watch how your real voice peeks out from behind its hiding place when you do. I wrote from my six year old voice and was excited to see the difference and simplicity in my writing.

Also, I want to encourage you to begin writing morning pages. Write everyday, whatever thoughts come into your head, *without* editing your words.

You'll be amazed at how it frees you up creatively and unlocks your unique voice.

Chapter Two

P ractice Writing

"I believe that what we want to write wants to be written. I believe that as I have an impulse to create, the something I want to create has an impulse to want to be born. My job, then, is to show up on the page and let that something move through me. In a sense, what wants to be written is none of my business." Julia Cameron

To get really good at anything we must put in the time. We must practice.

The dictionary defines practice this way: *to exercise or pursue as a profession, art, or occupation and to perform or do repeatedly in order to acquire skill or proficiency.*

In simple terms, it's doing something regularly until you get really good at it.

I was lucky enough to begin the discipline of practice when I was really young.

I began with piano lessons when I was five or six years old and started singing around the same time. It didn't take long until playing scales and learning new songs for thirty minutes a day became a habit. By the time I got into High School I was practicing two hours a day.

Even though I had a habit of practice in my life, learning to write and to master a new skill was difficult.

I think it's because I felt intimidated by all the other amazing writers out there. Many questions popped into my head as I began to practice writing everyday.

Would I ever be a published author? Would people even read or like what I had to say? How would I learn all that I needed to know about writing?

Those are the kinds of questions that bombarded my thoughts every time I sat down to write. Some days I'd only get a few words down, and other days I'd get more than 500 words a day which was a goal that I'd set for myself. But I did my best to write something as a consistent habit.

I kept at it.

Practice is just what it says. Doing something over and over again until you get real good at it.

Writing is something you practice.

Your writing gets better through repetition. The

words you put down on the page don't need to be perfect. You don't need to use big words or try to sound like anyone else.

The key to words that will draw new readers is for you to be your authentic self in whatever you write. This comes with practice. It's this consistency that helps you master the instrument that is you.

If you let yourself write consistently, you will become finely tuned like a singer who has been practicing scales for years.

Your words will become more expressive and flow with a greater fluidity and grace. Your words will become alive on the page and in the minds of your readers.

As you consistently practice writing everyday, you are building a bridge between who you are and the world.

If you think of your writing as a conversation with life, then you must bring to the conversation your entire self. Your attention, your thoughts and your flexibility in whatever words may come.

That's why writing is so amazing. Much like singing, there's a tension, an excitement and a spark of incredible possibility in what sounds may come out of you.

As you write daily, month after month and year after year, it brings a new freedom to the possibility of you.

It helps you discover new things in the world and opens your eyes to possibilities and adventures that are waiting.

Writing offers a gateway to touch something that is greater than ourselves. Writing is an act of love. It's a way of self-cherishing.

Writing rewards practice just as it does attention to detail. In order to write well we must practice being present and seeing the details all around us.

Since all of life is filled with drama, we can see interesting details all around us. Small moments have a large impact in the world around us. Our eyes, much like our ears, are trained to the smallest details by consistent attention.

The more we practice listening and seeing with close observation, the more we will gain an understanding of the possibilities and the nuances of emotional color and the black, white and greys that make up life.

It is noticing and writing out these details that makes us fall in love with writing over and over again.

Set Goals

"Even if there is a price to be paid, don't be afraid to use appropriate discipline. It may hurt in the short term, but it will pay dividends in the future." Coach John Wooden

Setting goals for yourself is important. With pretty much anything you really want to get done, you need to come up with some sort of plan.

This is the place, where you must choose. You can either control your own destiny or hand it over to circumstance. For myself, I'd much rather be actively doing something than reacting.

Being self-disciplined to work hard at the craft of writing and to continue to practice the fundamental principles is what will help you succeed.

It might seem like monotonous grunt work day after day, but you'll be happy with the results of making writing a habit. Not only will the book get finished and published, but you will have learned the valuable skill of steady practice.

Part of being self-disciplined is learning the art of perseverance. In art of any kind, or any sort of meaningful work, there seems to be more resistance against the artist. You need to work through the fear. You need to keep going in spite of it. You need to let fear be the indicator of your true north.

"Fear is good. Like self-doubt, fear is an indicator. Fear tells us what we have to do. Remember our rule of thumb: The more scared we are of a work or calling, the more sure we can be that we have to do it." Steven Pressfield in his book, *The War of Art.*

In other words, let the words that scare you the most be the ones you put on the page.

However, the words won't just appear on the page.

You need to plan when you'll create your own focused time to write.

Have you set a goal for yourself? I realized, after years of failure, that I needed to be specific with my goals in order to make something happen.

I struggled with goal setting for a couple years when I first started writing. That explains why in my early writing years, I only self-published one novel every three years. *Answering Annaveta*, was the first Book in the Historical Romance series was also the book that took me the longest time to write.

I didn't really have a goal, other than to keep writing. So some days I wrote and many days I didn't. It wasn't until I was working every week with an editor, that I really felt the push to stay on a schedule and get it done.

Since then I decided to try and stick closer to a schedule. I started with the goal of writing 500 words a day(for 6 days a week) then once that became quite doable, some days I would write 1000 words a day. I really believe that's why this book only took weeks to write.

Making that decision to have a quota or how many words you write a week is something that I learned from James Scott Bell. He says if you set a weekly goal, then even when the unexpected comes up in your week(which it always does) it is still doable to hit your goal by the end of the week.

That's why I set a goal to write between 3000 to

4000 words a week. Now, I don't always reach my goals and I don't aways work on on the same book.

I will often switch it up between the current fiction novel I'm writing and a new non-fiction book. I just do my best to get in my word count for each week.

The next step is to record your goals. Write them down on paper or type them into a computer file.

I keep a large paper calendar above my computer desk(which is in my bedroom) and that's where I write my word count for the day.

I also use a free cork board application on my computer where I can see the projects I'm working on.

Right now I have seven projects that are in various stages on the cork board. At the start of everyday when I look at my goals, it helps me to refocus and motivates me to keep writing.

The act of writing a goal and putting it somewhere where you see it everyday, helps to implant that goal firmly in your mind.

"There is one prevailing key to success. Do what you resolve to do. Then you'll be a success. If you can discipline yourself to follow through on your promises to yourself, your self-esteem goes up. Persistence is self-discipline in action. Self-discipline is the foundation of self-confidence ." ~ *Brian Tracy*

At that point, you'll want to write out your plan of

action. What steps do you need to take to get to your goal?

If you want to finish a book by December 31st, you can figure out how many words you'll have to write between now and then.

Next, divide that number by the number of weeks until the deadline. That's how you come up with your weekly quota of words that you need to reach.

Don't forget there might be research you need to include. Just think of the different steps you need and write them down. Check off the steps as you get them done, then repeat this process for every goal you have.

If you think about it in simple terms, it's really quite exciting. If all you write is 500 words a day, you'll have 15,000 words in 1 month's time and in 6 months you'll have a 90,000 word book finished.

That's two to three books a year that you could write and publish depending on the length of the book. How great is that? If you write only 500 words a day you're still writing more than many others who have wanted to write a book and didn't. So kudos to you. Keep it up.

That's the kind of thing I remind myself of when I want to quit(*yes, I have those kind of days too*). Many times I've got off track because I got caught in the cycle of reading blogs, articles and listening to podcasts about writing and self-publishing.

I've learned a lot from all that, but what I was really doing was procrastinating. I was just putting off the inevitable.

If you want to be a writer you have to write. And the beautiful thing is, the more you do it, the better your writing will become.

Something to try...

We talked about how vital it is to set your writing goals and commit to them.

So let's begin.

Observe what you do each day and write it down. Describe yourself and your tasks. Write with clear detail, a day in your life right now. Or look at yourself as a character in a novel. Describe the character that is you. This will help you practice observing details that are inside you and around you.

Next, write down a snapshot of ideas for books you would like to write. Then write down the date you want to see your book completed and published.

Then, write out a plan of action. What steps are you going to take to get to your goal? If your goal is to have your first draft finished in six months, you could set a 500 word count goal per day.

The last step is to decide how you're going to keep track of your goals. Put your target word count, where you can see it everyday.

Keeping track of your progress of daily or weekly quota of words on a large paper calendar works well. If you see your calendar when you sit down to write, it will help keep you inspired.

I have my calendar near my desk and computer where I see it everyday. Seeing it each day inspires me to keep writing. I hope it helps you too.

Chapter Three

C hoose What You Want to Write

"People who read want one of two things: knowledge or entertainment. When you can give them both, so much the better." James Scott Bell

Now you're ready to start brainstorming for your ideas.

Most likely if you're excited to write a book, you have one or maybe even several ideas of what you could write about. It's possible you have been thinking about that book idea for a while.

Consider the audience you'll be reaching with your book. Who are they and why do they read books?

There are two reasons people read books. To learn

something or to be entertained. If you can give them both so much the better.

If you have a fiction idea you would love to write, you have to remember that your first job is to entertain. It's not to get a message across. Movie mogul Samuel Goldwyn once said, "If you want to send a message try Western Union."

Your first job is to learn to tell a story readers won't want to put down. Everything else comes second for the novelist, because if readers don't want to read your book, it won't matter what your message is.

If you can add some knowledge that your reader would like to know about in your novels, that's even better.

For instance, in my historical romance novel *Anchoring Annaveta*, I share about the hero using a Brownie camera to take a picture of a terrorist in the novel. The Brownie camera was a new invention in the early 1900s.

These types of historical details add rich subtext to the story. Readers love to learn about these details and it fits together hand-in-glove with the romance and adventure in the story.

If you are writing non-fiction, people will buy your book because they want to learn how to do something, be something, or learn how to make more money or solve some kind of problem.

If you can give readers something they are looking for, be entertaining and if your voice or style also gives them enjoyment, then you will give readers amazing value.

Make it one of your goals to bring both entertainment and knowledge to every fiction and non-fiction book you write.

Now that we are in this brave new world of digital self-publishing, it's easier than ever to test the waters and try new things. You are only limited by how many words you decide to produce.

So how do you come up with ideas of what to write about? Ask yourself questions. Write down all the ideas that come into your head. Do a search on Amazon for topic ideas that you're excited about.

Maybe there's a skill or some sort of knowledge that you already have that people would love to learn about. Or maybe you have a story to tell that will inspire someone.

It was only when I brainstormed different topics that I got the idea to write this book. At some point in the near future I plan to create an online course that goes with this series of nonfiction books for writers.

My own years of struggle to write my first novel, gave me the passion to help others with their books.

Part of my story is that I searched for months reading many books on how to write a better novel, on editing and finally I learned all I could about how to format and upload your book onto Amazon and other platforms.

I also searched through blogs, podcasts and videos

trying to soak up all that I needed to know about writing and self-publishing.

I wanted to write this book to save people the time and frustration of needing to search for a really long time for the answers they were looking for on this topic.

A passion had grown inside me to somehow help others with a book and a course that I wish I had available to me when I first started writing and self-publishing.

A really great question to ask yourself as you are choosing what to write is: *Where does what I love to write meet an actual commercial possibility?*

In order to sell your books - if that's your goal - you need to combine what you're passionate about with what people are hungry to read.

If you are writing fiction... some of the most popular genres are: *romance, mystery, historical, thrillers, paranormal, science fiction, and fantasy.* You could choose one of those genres and do well at it.

As a writer, you should love what you're writing about, but you can also learn to love a specific genre.

That's what Nicholas Sparks did when he chose to write love stories that make people cry. He decided to go into writing with his eyes open as to what some of the bestselling genres were and he learned that each one had two big names that overshadowed the rest.

When the bestselling book *The Bridges of Madison County*, was released - a book written by a male author -

he decided he would start to write tear-jerking love stories.

If you are interested in literary fiction, that's great. You just need to be aware that literary fiction doesn't sell as well as commercial fiction genres.

So, as a writer, you get to choose what you want to write. If you are writing just for the love of writing or for the fun of a new challenge and don't need the added income, then write whatever you want to.

However, if your goal is to write as part of your living or to make a living as full-time writer, then it'll be helpful to look at what you love to write and combine that with what's selling right now.

See the world as it is, not through rose-colored glasses. To earn money writing, means taking time to research and understand what's going on in the market-place and the possibilities that are there.

Then armed with what you've learned, write books that have your own unique and authentic voice.

Define Your Passion and Purpose

"Make visible what, without you, might perhaps never have been seen." Robert Bresson

To get clear on your passion - which is what you want to write about - takes some focused thinking time.

I like to go to a room to think by myself for about

thirty minutes to ask myself a few questions and write down the answers.

For a non-fiction book I like to ask: *What topics would I love to write about? What knowledge do I have that could help others? What challenges did I have that I solved and how can those become lessons that will help others who are struggling with similar things? What do I know now that I wish I knew when I got started?*

For a fiction book the questions you ask will look a little different. *Who are the characters in my book? What is the big obstacle the hero or heroine is trying to overcome? What does your protagonist want? What does your antagonist want? Describe the setting for your story. If you are creating a unique story world, ask yourself what makes it unique?*

Writing down the answers to these questions will help you understand what you're really passionate about and help you get clear on the purpose for your book.

By knowing what your story is *really* about, you'll have clarity on what you want to communicate to your readers.

It's this conversation that creates your brand.

Now, the word 'brand' might make you cringe. You don't want to be a brand you want to be a person. You don't necessarily want to market to others, you want to share your story. You don't want *who you are,* to become a product you want to create art. I agree.

However branding isn't really about all of that. It's really about communicating to others.

To define your brand you need to really understand your own purpose, that of your audience and how you can connect the two. If you can't clearly define your purpose, then how can you engage your readers in a meaningful way?

One great way is to tell your story. In and of itself that engages people. Shape your story in a way that it relates to your work and share that when you meet people or write your story on the "About" page of your website.

This is about understanding your purpose as it relates to your writing, your goals and your audience. Too many writers give vague statements that could apply to thousands of writers.

You need to be specific and personalize your brand and consider how it connects with others in a meaningful way.

How is what you write different from other books in the marketplace?

You have to know what you are offering your readers that they can't get anywhere else. What you are writing and how you write it, needs to be unique in order to set your book apart from all the other books out there.

A great exercise that will help you understand this better, is to write some details about the topics you love to write about.

When I dug a little deeper into these questions, here's what I came up for my fiction: *"I write page-turning fiction about scarred girls who find who they are and discover strength they didn't know they had as they weather storms, push through obstacles and scary situations. I bring to these books a view about how love can grow even through tough circumstances. I base this on my God-given insight into human nature and my own experiences with becoming my authentic self and what I've learned about overcoming rejection to embrace belonging and love."*

You can do this with every genre you write in and with your non-fiction books too. Just have fun writing these ideas down and change them to suit you.

Share them with others and as you tweak your ideas, soon you'll have a brand - a unique selling proposition - that's uniquely you.

If you want, you can write something completely different by using a pen name.

Now, in the old days of only traditional publishing, an author would need to choose a pseudonym or pen name in order to write in another genre.

Bookstores didn't really know where to put your book if you as the author kept showing up in different genres. But all that changed with the introduction of the ebook. Now that we're in the digital world, many times authors no longer choose to use pen names.

I chose to use a pen name as sort of a test for myself. I wanted to see if my writing would be any different, if I wrote under a pen name. As it turns out, my writing voice is still the same no matter what name I use for my author name.

Readers quite often will find what you wrote in one genre and then they will cross over to the other books you've written because they like your style and your voice.

However it is still important to create an easily identifiable brand with your book cover and back blurb summary.

The most important step you can take is to keep writing. Continue to share your story. Connect your work and who you are with readers who will appreciate it most.

When you think about your identity as an author, consider framing your own story - these elements of branding - to help communicate who you are and what you write about to potential readers.

Once you've thought about what you are passionate about and you've answered the above questions, you're ready for the next step.

Create a Mind Map

Mind mapping is quite simple. It's basically a big brain dump on the page. Here's where you write down everything you know about a subject.

This is something I make use of when I write my nonfiction books.

To create a mind map, you start with the central topic in the middle of the page and then the spokes that lead out from your central topic, become the key points on that subject. As more ideas pop into your head, those details become the spokes.

You can make a mind map fun by adding different colors, drawing bubbles around the key points you want to make and the stories you want to tell. Essentially, you are just writing down everything you can think of about the book you want to write.

Structure isn't important at this stage. Most likely your mind map will look like a big mess of circles, phrases, words and arrows with a bunch of unfinished ideas. When you're at the start of the mind mapping process, how neat it is doesn't matter.

The most important thing is to keep writing down your ideas until you just can't think of anything else. Even if it sounds ridiculous, write it down. You never know if you'll use it or how it might spark another idea.

Please, don't restrict yourself on where you get your ideas.

Like author Suzanne Collins, you might be inspired by something on TV.

She told the media that she got the idea for *The Hunger Games* as she was switching between two channels. One of the channels had footage from the war in Iraq, and it got lumped together somehow with a popular reality TV show. The combination created the idea for an amazing bestselling book.

So think in terms of possibilities instead of placing limits on yourself.

Remember as you mind map, that you're not

creating an outline. Look at the next couple of chapters to get ideas on how to create an outline. This mind map you're creating is a way to get all the ideas that have been swimming around in your brain, written down onto the page.

When I created the mind map for this book, I used pencil and pencil crayons on blank computer paper. Doing that helped me get into a playful zone where the thoughts actually came faster.

There is something about writing by hand on paper that does that. Try mind mapping by hand, you'll be amazed at the results.

Once you have all your thoughts written down in a mind map, it's time to take those scrambled ideas that you've put on paper and make them organized.

In the next chapter, I'll give you tips on how to organize your mind map.

Something to try...

Take some time to think about your brand.

Write down the answers to these questions: *Why am I writing about these topics? At what point does my deepest passion meet my reader's greatest need? How can I share my story in a way that connects what I write with who I am?*

These answers will help frame your purpose and what you are bringing to the world.

Write down a paragraph of what you write. Describe what you want others to know about your writing that will simply and clearly help them understand the value you bring.

Now create a mind map and just write words and phrases that come to your mind about the topic you're excited to start writing about. It doesn't have to make sense right now. Just write it down.

I recommend creating a mind map using a pen or pencil and paper.

There's something about using good old-fashioned pen and paper that helps get the creative juices flowing.

When all your ideas are on the page, you're ready for the next step.

Chapter Four

Outline Your Book

You might be looking at your mind map right now and thinking, how am I going to make any sense of this?

If that's you, no worries. There's a way to clear up what seems chaotic and confusing.

Let's get into the steps.

First, arrange you mind map into categories, or groups.

Go through your mind map and choose which ideas seem to fit together into a group.

Then, once you have the ideas from your mind map sorted into separate categories, you'll see how each group of thoughts fits under a 'description.'

Depending on how many ideas you had, you might

have quite a few groups. For example, this book had twelve groups, which became twelve chapters.

Once you've grouped your ideas, you're ready to put them in a specific order for your book.

Lastly, you want to turn these individual groups into chapters.

So those are the simple steps to make sense out of your mind map. The rest of this chapter will talk about more tips that are specific for outlining fiction and non-fiction.

Here's a truth to remember as you write fiction or non-fiction. It's important to understand your audience. Both kinds of books are much easier and pleasurable for people to read when you add stories.

Telling stories can be great. By doing so, your audience can be educated, entertained and emotionally strengthened. Your readers can grow through shared experiences as they read your book.

Stories also bind communities together. So a huge priority in your mind as you write your book should be to consider what your audience wants and needs.

When you brainstorm and mind map first, it helps to flesh out the stories and ideas that your readers want to hear.

Once you've finished that, you're ready to dive into outlining. We'll tackle creating a fiction and nonfiction outline separately next.

. . .

Outline Your Fiction Story

In the world of fiction writers there are generally three kinds of writers.

The first is the seat-of-the-pants writer, or pantser or discovery writer who loves to just sit down and write and see where the story takes them.

Generally, pantsers don't really plan, eager to see what their writer's mind comes up with.

The second is the writer who likes to have the story all planned out in their mind before they write their novel. They preplan the story, figuring out an outline, characters and plot idea before writing.

They might even have index cards over their table or wall or if they use Scrivener, using the index cards for each scene.

The third type of fiction writer is one who combines the first two ideas. They do some preplanning - a sketch or an outline - and know the ending before they start, but after that, they write from the outline and still look for surprises in the scenes they write each day.

If you're the first type of writer, this chapter might not be very helpful for you. If you like to have a bit of a plan however, the next few paragraphs might give you some helpful insights.

The truth is that no matter what kind of novelist you are, when you've finished writing your manuscript, you will have a story - a plot. It might be a mess or a master-piece but it will be there staring you in the face.

The important question at that point will be does

this story connect with readers like it's supposed to? That's why reader's pick up a novel after all. They want to be transported and moved through the power of story. It takes a great plot to make that happen.

Either consciously or subconsciously, readers are asking: *What's the story about? What's happening? Why should I keep reading? Why should I care about these characters?*

These questions are answered best through a plot that is surprising and compelling. Most of the time, you can do this by creating a structured storyline - your plot.

One of the most popular books that has helped storytellers create their stories, is Joseph Campbell's book, *The Hero with a Thousand Faces.* Many characters from popular movies have been crafted based on this recipe, like *Katniss Everdeen, Harry Potter, Luke Skywalker,* and more.

However, the *Hero's Journey* should be used more like a lens to filter your story through, rather than a formula.

It's the character's journey that is somewhat like a cycle. The basic narrative pattern goes like this:

A hero goes from her ordinary world into an unknown world. As she continues on her journey, she goes through trials, failures, and meet with allies and enemies and gains growth and new skills. The hero, through her biggest struggle, gains revelation and insight and gets rid of her old self and accepts her new role. The hero begins the road back, wins the final challenge and enters a rebirth of sorts, with a new inner and outer freedom to claim the treasure she seeks.

I've outlined below the basic structure of the hero's journey that I hope helps you outline your story.

Act 1

1. The Ordinary World. This is the ordinary world in which your character lives. The hero is uncomfortable with the status quo and is introduced in a sympathetic way for the audience to identify with her situation or dilemma. Who the hero is, is shown against a background of environment, heredity, and personal history. Something in the hero's life is pulling her in different directions. The hero is stressed.

2. The Call to Adventure. Either external pressures or some kind **of internal pressure** shakes up the hero's situation. This is the point when the hero faces the beginnings of change.

3. Refusal of the Call. The hero, fearing the unknown, tries to turn away from the adventure... for a brief time. Another character might express uncertainty and the danger that lies ahead.

4. Hero meets with the Mentor. The hero meets up with a mentor who gives the hero training and advice that will help on the journey. Or it could be that the hero reaches inside herself to find a source of courage and wisdom.

5. Crossing the Threshold. The hero decides she is all in. At the end of Act One, the hero commits to leaving the Ordinary World to enter a new world or condition with new and unfamiliar rules and values.

Act 2

1. New Enemies, Allies and Trials. The hero faces disappointment about things that don't go as expected. The hero is tested as she tries to figure out who she can trust or not trust in this new world.

2. Preparation & Approach. The hero and her allies prepare to fight off their enemies in this new extraordinary world.

3. Crisis & New Growth. Near the middle of the story, the hero becomes part of the central space in this extraordinary world. She confronts death and faces her greatest fear. From this moment of death, comes a new life.

4. Gets the Treasure. The hero gets the treasure won by facing his or her fears and or death. The hero accepts their new role. Here's where the victory party is, but the hero also faces the danger of losing the treasure again.

5. The Result. At about the three quarter mark in

the story, the hero is compelled to complete the adventure. She leaves the extraordinary world she's been in, to bring the treasure home. This is often the place where a chase scene signals the urgency and danger of the mission.

Act 3

1. The Hero's Rebirth & Return. At the climax of the story, the hero is severely tested once again on the threshold of home. The lie they have believed seems overwhelming. Your hero's worst fears have come true. She is cleansed by a last sacrifice, another moment of death and rebirth, but on a higher level. Because of the hero's courage to take action, the conflict that she grappled with in the beginning is finally settled.

2. The Hero Returns with Treasure. Your hero has an epiphany. The main character finally realizes the truth. It sets her free from the lie she's hung onto. The hero storms the castle and fights for the truth that she's found and begin to work at figuring out how to win and get to her goal. She's attacked by lies, but holds onto the truth.

3. Resolution. All the tangled plot lines get straightened out.

4. Back to the Ordinary World. Your hero seizes the day and gets to her perfect ending. Status quo is upgraded to a new level for the hero. Nothing is quite the same again, once you're a hero.

This basic structure of the hero's journey has been used to make bestselling movies and books.

I've found this structure to be helpful to glance at when I'm writing as a guide. Its use is more like having a story coach at your side giving you tips when you need them.

After you've roughly sketched out what happens in the above three Act structure, your next step is to write story beats.

Story beats are basically a paragraph explaining what's going on and what's going to happen in that chapter.

Write your beats with the idea that you're predicting what will happen rather than your writing down what must happen.

That way, you will have a lot of flexibility if suddenly your story wants to take you in a different direction than you originally planned. If you decide to use story beats, remember they are more like guideposts not required plot elements.

When you can be flexible in writing your beats, then you are letting your characters be what they want to be so they can organically find their way. That way you'll end up with the best of both worlds: amazing characters combined with a compelling and clear story.

So go ahead and start filling in the blanks of this three act structure and work on your beats. You'll be amazed how quickly the story idea that was lingering in your head, becomes fleshed out when you combine the two.

You'll have a solid story from beginning to end, which means it will be easier than ever to write it quickly.

Outline Your Non-Fiction Book

Great non-fiction, like fiction, tells a story. Often it includes a story from the author of how they did this or that or maybe it includes stories of others.

I've included stories of other writers and a little of my own story in this book.

When you tell detailed stories in your non-fiction book, it helps readers to follow and learn from the information you're giving them.

Stories help readers to digest content at a much faster pace so they can apply what they are learning to their own lives.

However when you're writing non-fiction, rather than writing story beats, it's best to think in terms of an outline.

As you write your outline, write down what your readers need and want to know. Make a list of the main points and ask yourself what topics you could cover under each of them to explain those points.

Keep narrowing down each point and look for the

best examples, until you drill down to the basics of your topic.

Next, be flexible as you write adding more details or stories as necessary.

Below I share the details of the original outline for this book:

Introduction. Some inspiration for first-time writers who have dreamed of writing a book, but have felt stuck because of resistance like fear, insecurity and other forms of resistance.

Chapter 1. Why You Should Write Your Book Now

Main Point. The benefits of writing your book

First Point. Unlock your creativity with practice. Write from your gut. Practice morning pages.

Chapter 2. Practice Writing

First Point. The art of practice. Writing is a conversation. Learn to listen within and around you. Noticing details will help you become a better writer.

Second Point. Goal setting. Being disciplined to set daily or weekly word count that works for you.

Chapter 3. Choose What You Want to Write

First Point. People read for knowledge or entertainment. If you give your readers what they're looking for, you're giving your readers amazing value. Tell my story of searching Google for related blogs, articles and reading tons of books to understand better how to write and publish my first book.

Second Point. Talk about defining your brand. It's how you communicate to others. Your identity as an author and how you frame your own story.

Chapter 4. Outline Your Book

First Point. How to Outline Your Fiction Story. The basic structure to write a compelling story. Writing story beats can help you write your story faster.

Second Point. How to Outline Your Non-Fiction Book. Non-fiction is still about story telling because that draws the reader in.

And so on...

That's an example of how I outlined the first few chapters of this book. If you look in the table of contents of this book, you'll see what I did.

There's also another way a non-fiction book can be outlined. You can simply have a major idea per chapter and write a summary for each chapter.

This is a more narrative way of outlining. It's a little more like a story.

This is similar to Malcolm Gladwell's style of writing. He tells his nonfiction through stories.

Either style of writing works well and no matter which method of outlining you use, the structure stays the same. There's the main points with examples and explanations that go deep enough to explain what you're trying to say.

Preparing and planning what you want to say is very important for this kind of writing. The better you know your topic, the faster you'll write.

When you have a detailed outline in place for all the points you're trying to make, then you'll be able to write your first draft quickly.

The only other detail to remember is that you'll need to research all the information that you're unsure about. The keys to writing good non-fiction is that research is critical.

There may be many points that you need to verify or look up if you're not sure about the answer. It's great that we have the Internet and so many books that help us do that.

Those are the basics on how to outline your non-fiction book. I hope it helps you to write your own book.

The important key when you are writing either fiction or non-fiction is to write your first draft as fast as you can. What I mean by that, is try not to make your first draft perfect.

If you overthink every word, phrase or paragraph you'll end up doubting yourself, over editing and basically second-guessing yourself all the way through.

If you do that, your chances of getting creatively blocked are very high. We all have an over-developed inner critic that nags at us no matter what we're writing.

Shoo that nasty creature out of the room and focus on getting your words written.

Something to try...

The first step is to arrange the mind map you created into categories, or groups. Go through your mind map and choose which ideas seem to fit together into a group.

Then, once you have the ideas from your mind map sorted into separate categories, you'll see how each group of thoughts fits under a *description.*

You might have 4, 7, 11 groups. It doesn't matter how many. Just group your ideas until all your separate ideas are in a group.

Now that you have separate groups, you should be able to sketch out what you would call each one. These will become your chapters. And you can organize which chapter comes first, second and so on.

If you are writing a fiction story, begin right now to write short two to three sentence story beats for each chapter until you get to the end.

Don't overthink it.

Just write your ideas out as fast as you can. You'll be surprised at how quickly your outline comes together.

If you are writing a non-fiction book, choose which style of book you are writing. Is it more narrative and does your writing have stories with explanations and details thrown in?

Then you might find it easier to outline by writing a

paragraph summary describing briefly what you want to focus on in each chapter.

If your non-fiction book is more about how-to, with a ton of information and details, then you might consider using a similar outline to the one above.

The most important key is that you begin to write your outline today.

Chapter Five

Write Your First Draft Quickly

"Almost all good writing begins with terrible first efforts. You need to start somewhere." Anne Lamott, Bird by Bird

Many times we hesitate because of fear, when we write our first draft.

Fear is one of toughest things to push past as a writer. At least that has been true for me.

I remember when I wrote my first novel. I would sit there and stew about each and every word, phrase and paragraph.

Sometimes I would get up and pace, trying to find the right word. I didn't realize the harm I was doing to my creative flow.

When I started out, I was scared of sharing my words and of failing at one of the things I truly loved. The fear didn't go away, like I thought it would after I finished my first novel.

I continue to write and I've continued to feel this fear of both failure and success - or more to the point, the expectations that come with it and the fear of someone telling me you're not a *real* writer.

I've talked with other writers and they tell me the fear never really goes away. Fear is still there, but you learn how to take action anyway.

A blogger friend of mine, Jonathan Milligan once told me, *movement brings clarity*. So when you act despite the forms of resistance that show up trying to block your progress, you get clearer vision.

Here's something I've noticed. That thing you fear to write the most is your guide to where you should focus your attention.

There's a reason it seems scary to write about that topic and you must follow that resistance you are feeling like a compass, toward writing those words that you are most afraid to write.

Steven Pressfield in his book *The War of Art,* says it best:

"Rule of thumb: The more important a call or action is to our soul's evolution, the more Resistance we will feel toward pursuing it." Steven Pressfield

When you take action to master fear by admitting it, naming it and taking action in spite of it, you'll push past fear every time.

This is the sort of resistance you will face, especially as a first time writer. Your first draft of your very first book, will ask a ton of courage from you.

When you write that first draft, you can't insist your writing be perfect. First-draft perfection is impossible. Not only that, but by constantly switching from your creative brain to you editing brain, you are slowing down your own progress.

Your creativity is a right brain function and editing is a left brain function. When I had that *aha moment,* it changed the first draft writing process for me.

As I wrote the first draft of the second book in my Historical Romance series, the writing went much faster because I wasn't constantly looking over every single word. I've continued to learn from my mistakes.

What you can do instead is to keep your mind map and the outline you made close beside you as you type on the computer. *Use creative action to bury your fear.*

When I wrote my first novel and again as I write this book, I wrote my chapter outlines on index cards and laid them all out.

It not only helped me to see where I was headed, but the act of writing out each chapter and the details that went with it, helped the fear get pushed to the wayside.

Another thing that I was inspired to do after

listening to podcasts from indie authors like Joanna Penn, Mark Dawson and others was to write inspirational quotes and keep them where I could see them everyday as I write.

So basically the top part of my desk is littered with quotes that remind me of my vision and why I write. I hope you surround yourself with quotes or pictures that encourage you to keep creating too.

So let's get to the part where you take action.

HERE ARE SOME BASIC GUIDELINES TO HELP YOU WRITE YOUR FIRST DRAFT.

The First Draft is not supposed to be perfect.

Don't worry if you don't have a fully formed book when you write your story or book for the first time.

These words are allowed to be not so great and very often are. It's meant to be so. To create a perfectly formed sentence on the page, to be followed by another right out of the shoot, is expecting too much of yourself. That's not how writing works.

Michael Crichton said it best. *"Writing is rewriting."*

Remember that, and then go write your epic novel or non-fiction first draft that you can shape into something magnificent later.

· · ·

Set A Word Count Goal. Like I mentioned in Chapter two, it's really helpful and motivating to set goals on how many words you'll write each day.

I usually aim for 500 words a day. But I started at 250 words.

It was all I could do when I was first starting out. Soon, I got that word count up to 500 and then when I was writing that consistently six days a week, I was able to move that up to 1000 words a day for short bursts of time.

I learned to do this when I did my first NaNoWriMo(National Novel Writing Month) in November of 2011. The word count goals helped me move a lot faster than I would have, if I wouldn't have set any goals.

The thing is, if you don't have some kind of goal, you won't achieve anything. I really believe that. Having a plan also breaks the work down into manageable chunks.

The exciting thing is that if you were writing a novella or a shorter ebook that was 30,000 words, if you wrote just 500 words a day you'd have the first draft done in 60 days.

If you were writing a full length novel that was around 80,000 words, if you wrote 500 words a day you would have the first draft done in 160 days or a little over 5 months.

Of course you'd still need to edit, but you can't edit a blank page. So go ahead, set your word count goal and start writing.

. . .

Use a Writing Software that Helps You Focus.

There are many ways you can write your story. You can use different kinds of software like Scrivener, Word or Google docs or others. You could even write your story by hand.

Personally, I love using *Scrivener* to write. It really has changed my writing life, and made it easier. When you use this software you'll discover amazing productivity tools.

You can set Project Targets, so if your book will be approximately 50,000 words and you set your Session Target at 500 words, every time you sit down to write, you can have those targets floating at the bottom of your writing document. You'll see the progress bar move and it motivates you to keep writing.

I also like to use Compose Mode in Scrivener. You can fill your whole screen with a blank document or you can put the picture of your book cover as the background, which is really inspiring.

Using Compose Mode in Scrivener really helps to get rid of distractions, so you can focus as you write.

HERE ARE A FEW HELPFUL TIPS TO GET MORE WRITING DONE.

Tip number one: Set a Timer for a more focused Writing Session. I will often use a count-down timer(*you can search for that on Google search*).

Knowing you have a time limit in which to get your words written really helps you stay focused. Even if you start with 10 or 15 minutes, it will help you get going on your writing project.

The important thing is not to get distracted during that time. Don't check the Internet or any social media or even make yourself a cup of coffee or tea. When the timer is set, you write. It's that simple.

I can't tell you how much this has helped me to to get my word count done each day. It's really been invaluable.

Tip number two: Get up early. I get up at 5:30am almost everyday. I start with meditation and then I write three morning pages. Usually I'm ready to write by 6am if not before. I write best when my brain is still half asleep.

A writer friend of mine, Stacy Claflin, gets up a 4am every morning to write and already she has written an amazing amount of books in a relatively short amount of time.

I think the early morning helps because your mind isn't so polluted by everything that has happened in the day. Your internal critic or editor is still fast asleep. That's a very good thing when you're trying to get the first draft written.

However, you'll need to discover how you work best.

Maybe instead of being a morning person, you're a night owl and love to write when everyone else is fast asleep. That's great. Plan to write during that time. You'll probably get a lot more done.

The point is, find time that you don't normally have to get your writing done. It is such a good feeling when you finally discover your groove and start being consistent with your goals.

You begin to feel like you are becoming the great writer you know you can be. Steven Pressfield calls this *Turning Pro* in his very helpful book titled: *Turning Pro: Tap Your Inner Power and Create Your Life's Work.*

Tip number three: Cut down your TV time. I cut it down to one hour a night - on the nights I watch TV - and after that I work on other things like a blogpost or write in a project I currently have going. It really helps to begin to schedule your time, so you can get a lot more writing done.

Of course, it's important to have a strategy. When you choose the best workflow that works for you, you will get more books finished in a shorter amount of time.

Strategy for Writing

Stephen King, in his fantastic book titled**,** *On Writing,* says that you can approach writing with excitement, nervousness, hopefulness or even in a state of despair that you'll never be able to completely put on the page what's in your mind and heart.

He goes on to say that you can come to the blank page any way but lightly. When you take writing seriously, you'll see your efforts rewarded.

One thing that helps each of us as writers is to read a lot. It's important because it creates an ease and intimacy with the process of writing.

Endless reading will pull you into a place where you can write without self-consciousness. It also helps you to grow as a writer. By reading a lot you'll learn the words and phrases that have been overused and you'll understand what is fresh language.

Your first draft, whether it's fiction or non-fiction should be written as fast as you can do it. That way the characters and ideas stay fresh in your mind.

If you go too many days between writing, you'll find that your ideas begin to sound stale and your enthusiasm disappears, just a little. That's pretty much the kiss of death for any writer. So be consistent and write a little almost everyday.

Something I've heard a lot of writers say is that they work best in a peaceful atmosphere. I've definitely found that to be true. Days when I've had a lot of *solid talks*(my way of saying heated discussions) with my husband or sometimes my children, those are the days I don't get a lot of words written.

So a stressful atmosphere does not help you to write

your book. Do your best to find that peaceful place even if you have to go to the basement to do it.

I write at my desk in my bedroom. More often then not, the shades are pulled down, because I tend to get too distracted otherwise. I put the productivity music on and start writing. I know that if I want to get the word count in for that day, I need as few distractions as possible.

Write what you love to read is really one of the greatest tips I can give a new author. If you love reading romances or sci-fi, then write that. If you've had a longing to write your memoir, then by all means, write that. I'm sure there will be many people who would love to hear your story.

A really good guideline is to write what you like and then breathe life into your words by blending your own personal knowledge of life, friendship and work into it.

If your book is non-fiction, don't shy away from writing about work. People love to read about work.

Use what you know to sweeten the story. Tell the truth of what you know and spin your tale around that, and you'll leave readers hungry for more.

Choose Your Workflow

Workflow is important, because as humans we love routine.

If someone is starting a new diet and they want to workout everyday, just by starting each day with small steps will help them reach their goal. This is similar to writing.

Since this is a new routine you are forming, it might help you to start with small habits:

First day: go to the computer and open up a document, sit down and choose your writing music.

Second day: at the same time as the day before, go back to your computer, sit down, turn on your music, and open a document. Write a sentence.

Third day: go to your computer(at the same time), sit down, put your music on, open your document and start writing with a goal of 100 words.

If each day you repeat a routine similar to the one above, you will soon get in the habit of going to your computer and writing each day.

And if you stick to writing your word count goal - maybe starting with 250 words a day - then you'll soon be in a routine that will help you reach your goals faster.

As you are writing your first draft, do it with the door closed. Write like you mean business and don't let anyone see your first draft until it's finished so they won't be able to influence you as its forming.

Don't worry how your first draft comes out. If it's a messy version with a bunch of grammatical errors or weird sounding phrases, it doesn't matter.

The job of the writer in the first draft is to get the words out there. To just say what you need to say.

In the second draft, you are ready for revisions. This

is when you write words that say what you mean - words that make sense out of the first draft.

That's the beautiful thing about the rewriting process. This is often the place where the real story emerges out of what can be a *cluttered and confusing* first draft. Rewrite until you feel like the story is flowing how you want it to.

After your fiction story or non-fiction book sounds like it's flowing how you want it to, you're ready to write a third and final draft.

This is where you will rewrite your second draft until it's like a shiny new penny. This is the polishing stage. It's your chance to fine-tune your language and your scenes, which really makes your story sparkle with simplicity and clarity.

Remember to never stop learning how to improve your writing craft. Use great descriptions. It's the details of what's going on in your story that helps the reader be transported there.

It's a learned skill that comes by reading a lot and writing a lot. As you read you'll learn how much description to add to your scenes and as you write you'll learn how to craft your sentences in a way that sparks your readers' imagination.

Description starts with your imagination and an understanding of what you want the reader to experience. Then your job is to bring what you see to the page. The more you do it, the better you'll get at it.

The goal, is to be able tell your story, so your reader's

'arm hairs stand on end' with awareness of what you're saying. So do a lot of practice and remind yourself that your job is to say what you see and share the emotions you feel, as you tell your story.

Once you begin your routine and are committed to a distraction free workflow, you'll have set yourself up to be productive in your writing time each day.

Something to Try...

To begin writing your first draft, put your mind map - with its grouped sections - close by the computer.

Turn on your music(*if you like music*).

Set a timer for 10 to 15 minutes. You can use your phone, a portable kitchen timer or whatever you like. I use a countdown timer that I found on Google that works well for me.

Open your document and begin writing. Remember during this time period, you aren't checking email, social media or answering the phone. It's your time. You get to write something.

Leave your inner critic out of the room. You don't need him or her.

Visualize the story you have in your head and just begin.

Don't stop until you've hit your goal. If you want to start with 300 words, that's great. If you only have 100 words done by the time the timer buzzes, take a 5 minute break. Come back to your computer after 5 minutes and set the timer again for 25 minutes and continue writing.

Keep doing this until you've hit your target goal for the day.

You'll feel so productive when you've hit your goal for the day.

Next step: Stay committed to writing the words each day until your story is finished. You'll boost your confidence as a writer when you do.

Chapter Six

Your Book Cover Image and Title

Now that you've finished editing your book you are almost ready to put your masterpiece out into the world.

However, there are a few important steps still to go that matter a lot to potential readers. That is your book cover and book title.

A fantastic cover is a huge selling point. Beyond word of mouth, recommendations, and great reviews, your cover is what sells your book.

Your book cover image needs to show up on your website or other digital stores, or as a print copy and look so good that readers will want to pick it up.

.   .   .

Book Cover Image

As an indie author, you have the freedom to decide your own book cover.

A beautiful book cover can increase your own excitement to finish writing your book and get it out into the world.

However, sometimes it's the endless time spent searching stock photos and the struggle to get the right concept for your book cover that can drive you around the bend.

I often get a little unnerved when choosing a book cover image. I think I'm on edge because I know the influence a good cover(or bad cover) has on book sales, so I not only need to figure out a great cover, but also need to pay a book designer or figure out a way to get it done right. *The truth is that a book cover - done well - will almost always pay for itself.*

Maybe you won't sell 100 or 200 copies of your book right away, but more than likely you will at some point.

Which means your book cover will have paid for itself. Having a good book cover is a big part of having a good product that readers will want.

Your book cover is the first thing a potential reader will see. It's your big chance to catch someone's eye and pull them in for a closer look.

Then as they look at your product description and book title, those two items should do the hard work of convincing them to buy your book.

But what was the reason they picked up your book or clicked on the thumbnail version of your book, on *Amazon, Kobo or any other digital store? More than likely, it* was the book's cover.

Essentially, your book cover is the biggest marketing asset your book has.

It's important to make your book cover the best it can be. At the very least, you don't want readers to look at your book cover and mentally disregard your book just because it looks like some other not-so-great "self-published" book covers that are out there.

Many of the self-published book covers of indie authors I know are really awesome, but there are a few... well you know. It is really worth the time, effort and cost to get it right.

Something to remember as you begin brainstorming for book cover ideas is that if you aren't sure you can do a good job on your book cover, it might be best to hire a graphic design artist.

If you're not sure where to look for someone to design your book cover, check out 99Designs.com Usually the basic range for a professional cover is around $250 to $500. This is a normal price range for a good book cover.

When choosing a book designer, look at work they've done before. See if your friends have any recommendations. See if what they create is compatible with your genre and if their prices are in your budget.

However, if it's not in your budget, you can get a

designer on Fiverr.com to create a book cover for you for just a few dollars.

Or if you have an idea of what you want and have a working knowledge of Photoshop, you can work on it yourself or ask a friend who is good at graphic design.

Maybe you live near an Art College. Art students are always working on building their portfolios and many would jump at the chance to create a book cover for a small fee.

If you are working with someone else, agree upon a completion date and how many revisions the artist will allow.

Then you'll have a chance to suggest changes to the design to make sure you are satisfied with the end result. This is what I did with my first book cover. I was quite happy with how it looked when it was done.

A place to start is to spend some time analyzing the book covers in your chosen genre. Look at the book covers of the top ten best sellers in your genre. What colors stand out? How did they place the images? Is there a theme in your chosen genre?

Choose a photo that either symbolizes what your book is about or conveys the mood. You really want to pique your reader's curiosity.

When I was choosing the book cover for my first historical romance, I knew that genre consistently had pictures of women on the front cover. I wanted to convey the genre as soon as a reader saw the thumbnail image of my book.

Remember, your book cover is for the reader, not for you. The image you choose needs to transfer genre and concept to potential readers. It's really great if your readers talk up your book covers and tell all their friends.

If you have a bad cover, it will stop readers from picking up your book. Or the few that still read your story, might tell their friends *never mind how this book cover looks, the story is really good.*

I want to encourage you, not to let that happen to you. On an encouraging note, because you've self-published your book, you can always re-publish with a better book cover, if your first one isn't doing too well.

So here are some practical tips as you begin to choose the cover for your new book.

If want to make your own book cover, there are some websites where you can do this with very little money. I have a writer friend who uses diybookcovers.com and she creates great book covers.

I've tried using Canva.com and that is a great option that's simple to use. So I've been looking at this option for one of my next book releases.

Or you can create your book cover with Photoshop if you know how. I really recommend you have some design experience though, if you are going to try making your own book cover.

To find royalty-free photos look at places like bigstockphoto.com, dreamstime.com or depositphotos.-

com. However, you need to keep in mind that you don't own the image. You are just paying to use it.

The image belongs either to the website where you got it or the photographer. Start by teaching yourself about the important concepts for a good book cover by looking at bestselling book covers in your genre as well at blogposts at websites like thebookdesigner.com.

There are some creative and strategic ways to place photos on your book cover. For example, you can include a box or colored band where you place your book title.

You can see what my graphic designer did with my first book *Answering Annaveta*. She put the photo of the girl at the top and then just added a matching green box to put the title of the book inside.

What you might not realize is that the photo of the girl and the bottom photo of the large Russian house, are separate pictures. I thought it all blended together quite nicely.

If you want to get a closer look at that book cover example, just go to lornafaith.com/books. You can make something like that work for your book too.

After you have your book cover image worked out, your next step will be to choose your book title.

Book Title

After you've created a professionally designed book

cover that draws your readers in visually, you need to write a book title that speaks to them and hooks them.

Your book title needs to stand out. When you upload your ebook onto a website or Amazon or any other digital platform, your book title needs to be easily readable as a thumbnail image. So it's critical to choose an easy-to-read typeface or font that is large enough to read.

Look at other bestselling books in your genre to see what font they're using, and consider using something similar. Part of the reason they are bestselling books is because they've learned which type of picture and font to use for the cover.

A great, free source for fonts can be found at fontsquirrel.com. Another good source, that is more budget friendly, is myfont.com.

You want your book title to perk your readers eyes long enough to earn a serious look at your back cover blurb. This is most reader's last stop before they decide if they will buy your book.

For fiction books, the goal of a good title should create curiosity. Along with the cover of your book, your title should give your potential reader a sense of what the book is about.

I know when I read the back cover of a fiction book my inner ear is listening for tone and what kind of reading experience I'll get if I buy it. I don't know if that's just me because of my musical background, but there is somewhat of a musical sound that I hear when I read titles of fiction books.

There's a different sound between a warm romance tone, the serious thriller or the curiosity that a Science Fiction book title gives me.

My first novel, *Answering Annaveta,* is about a girl who is becoming a woman. Through all the abuse from her father and as she faces other tragedies she is trying to figure out who she is. She is searching for answers.

So, the title gives a glimpse into her dilemma and the real theme of the story. I was trying to build curiosity for potential readers.

As you brainstorm possible book titles, dig deeper into the theme of your story. Try it out on family and friends and see what their initial reactions are.

For non-fiction books, you're looking for a title that can be combined with a subtitle that brings clarity to what your book is about and tells readers what benefit they will get when they read it.

You want readers of your non-fiction book to look at your title and be able to say to themselves *that's the answer I was looking for.*

One way to find a great title for your book is to do some simple keyword research. At it's most basic, a keyword is something that a person types into a search engine(*like Google*) when they're looking for information.

When you do a little bit of research on popular words or phrases and use them in your own book title, it can really give your book a boost. More people will see your book in their search engines.

Most people don't realize it, but Amazon is also a search engine. The only real difference between Google and Amazon is that on Amazon people are ready to buy your book when it shows up in the search engine.

So that is good news.

To figure out how to best use this technique, you can use the Google search engine, like I did, and search for something like "how to find keywords for your book." You will find a variety of blogs, podcasts and videos that show you how to find good keywords for your book.

The key with non-fiction titles is to try to see what your readers will be searching for and then do your best to answer the questions readers will have about your topic in your title or subtitle.

Ideally your book title is meant to make whatever benefit you're giving the reader, very clear to those who are an ideal fit for it.

In the end, your book needs to stand out. A compelling book cover and title are what will grab their attention.

Something to Try...

Start by choosing which way you're going to go with the book cover.

If you decide to go with a graphic designer, consider

99Designs.com. The nice thing about using 99Designs is that they'll create quite a few mock-up covers which are created by different designers when trying to impress a client. Then you as the author pick your favorite.

It's fun to post the picture of your potential book cover on social media and ask your friends which book design they like best too.

You can also check out book designers on Fiverr.com. Many times, you can get a decent book cover for less than $20.

Do a search of images that you like at the some of the websites listed above for photos you like and then once you've purchased them you can pass the photos along to your designer.

Or if you want to do it yourself, check out DIYBook-Covers.com or Canva.com. It takes a little bit of trial and error, but once you've got it figured out, then it doesn't take long to get your book cover image done. If you want, you can learn simple steps on how to create a good book cover using Canva by reading this blogpost on my website for writers: https://www.createastoryy oulove.com/9-simple-steps-to-create-a-book-cover-using-canva/

Once you have your book cover, brainstorm titles. Talk it over with friends and beta readers too if you want suggestions for a good book title. Remember you want a title that grabs the reader.

Start by doing a search on Google for great book

titles, especially if you're writing non-fiction. For fiction, it's great to have a title that draws curiosity.

Do some brainstorming and then check with a few people whose opinions you value online or offline and see what their gut reaction is.

Once you have your book title and book cover done, your front cover is done.

Chapter Seven

Tips on Formatting, Back Cover Blurbs and Pricing Your Book

In this chapter I'll talk about tips for formatting your book, writing your back cover product description and pricing your ebook and print book.

I'm just going to go over a few details like file types here and how to create your cover and table of contents.

The way I figured out how to format, was by learning from Joseph Michael's amazing online course *Learn Scrivener Fast*. I highly recommend it. If you don't have Scrivener software it's the best(*in my opinion*) software out there for writers.

The *Learn Scrivener Fast* course has been my go-to tutorial to help me understand formatting and compiling my ebooks.

Another helpful book that gives detailed explanations on formatting and compiling is *Scrivener for Dummies* by Gwen Hernandez.

Formatting

If you've chosen to go with Scrivener as your writing software, then this chapter will help you.

If you want another option that you can use to format your ebook for free, check out www.calibre-ebook.com.

For myself, I find Scrivener the best software to write in and one of the easiest to self-publish with. Formatting with Scrivener is all done during the "compile" process. It's fairly simple to learn.

In the past few years however, I've started using another eBook and print book software called Vellum. It really does create beautiful eBook and print books.

Yes, you read that right. It creates print books too! How great is that? If you want to create both unlimited ebooks and print books, you can learn more about Vellum and how to format your book using Vellum in this tutorial here: https://www.createastoryyoulove. com/vellum/

I self-published this book using Vellum and it's super simple to do. That's really great news for you as you write and publish your first book.

As a writer, your main focus should be on how to write more words, instead of spending hours and days worrying about how to figure out the subheadings of each chapter and other stuff.

What template should I use?

If you are using Scrivener to write and format your eBook, it will be simpler to do if you create your ebook using the Novel template.

Whether your book is fiction or non-fiction this is the best template to use. It will save you a bunch of headaches later, if you start here.

The novel template is better because it already has a place for your book cover, a title page, copyright, dedication and acknowledgements.

Next, depending on your book, you might want to include a series page or an 'other books' by this author page. There's also a spot to put your blurb page, where other authors or reviewers say wonderful things about your writing.

There's also an author page where you say a little something about yourself - a short bio - and point to your website and social media channels.

If you've been using Scrivener, but have written your text in a different template it's easy to switch.

Just start a brand new project in Novel template and copy and paste your text from the previous writing software into the new template on Scrivener.

· · ·

Which file type do you need?

In Scrivener you can compile for kindle(.mobi) format; you can compile for Nook, iBookstore and Kobo(.ePub) format and you can compile for Smashwords or Draft2Digital.

When I first started self-publishing books, I needed to learn how to compile two main file types to publish ebooks. A couple years ago, Amazon Kindle changed their requirements on digital book files from .mobi files to .epub files.

This makes it a lot easier to compile and publish your books on all digital retailers.

For formatting your ebook, you can find 'compile' when you go to the main menu and click on File > Compile in Scrivener.

Or if you are using Vellum to format your ebooks, when you click on *Generate* you can choose the specific digital retailer that you need.

How do you add Chapter Headings?

You can turn your text document into a page that has titles for chapters, and subsection headings when you use the "Formatting" section of the "Compile" panel.

It's quite handy, because you can choose whether that passage of text has Chapter One at the top(*or if you want, you can give it a title instead*). You can choose whether that's included or not.

When Scrivener compiles the ebook, you can choose the settings so that you have one or two blank lines at the top of each page, then have "Chapter One" and under that write your title.

Then you can reset the settings so that it gives you another blank line under that before the story actually begins.

What do I do about my Table of Contents and Book Cover?

The beautiful thing is that Scrivener does it for you. There's a "Cover" section that's similar to the "Formatting" section mentioned above.

All you need to do here is drag your cover image into the Scrivener file and choose it for this section. Normally this file is 800X600 pixels, and is bundled into your ebook file.

Something to remember, is that this cover won't be the same cover you'll upload to display on book sites. It's much smaller.

As for your table of contents, Scrivener automatically includes the table of contents that you wrote down when you used the Novel template. It's that simple.

Back Cover Blurb

The back cover blurb is also known as your product

description. When you write your book, you give certain promises to your reader.

Holly Lisle says, that "ALL fiction promises are the equivalent of ensuring an open airway in trauma triage. If your patient does not have(*or get*) an open airway, you cannot save him. If you do not fulfill ALL fiction promises, you cannot save your book."

So your title and book cover, whether its non-fiction or fiction - makes a promise to the reader that the narrative inside needs to deliver on.

When you write your back cover blurb you are writing a teaser or description copy about your book's plot(fiction) or the solution you're offering(nonfiction).

As you write your blurb, it's helpful to keep foremost in your mind, what the reader of your book is looking for. It's a little easier to figure that out for nonfiction readers, as they picked up your book looking for a solution to a problem or question in their life.

So your description would convey that promised solution and then give a few points on the contents of your book.

Readers of fiction are looking for an emotional experience and hook - something that will pique their interest - without spoiling anything.

Look at the back cover blurbs of the top selling books in your genre or find some movie trailers to get an idea on how to write this copy well.

Here's another tip that might be helpful. Do you

best to hook the reader within the first two or three lines of your product description.

Most readers are just casually glancing through books and aren't interested in taking a long time to read the back cover.

One of the reasons I want to learn to write my blurbs better is simply because I want to respect my reader's time.

By reading through those lines, the reader will have a good idea what your book is about and if it's their kind of book, they'll already be sold on it.

Pricing Your Book

If you are going the self-published route for your book, then you have control over the price of your book.

If you are going with a traditional publisher than this is not your decision, but it's important either way to know about price points.

Pricing a ebook, seems to be an area where most authors test to see what works for them. From books I've read by successful indie authors, the consensus seems to be to price your fiction book between $2.99 and $5.99 for the sweet spot for sales. For myself $4.99 has been a good price point for my historical romance and my pen name sweet romance series.

For your first book, look at what best selling books are going for in your category or niche. What is your market happy to pay for this type of book?

Amazon's royalty structure is that you as the author earn 70% on books that are priced between $2.99 - $9.99 for specific markets and 30% for books that are priced over $9.99 or under $2.99.

Remember, that when you price your ebook at $2.99, your 70% royalty is $2 which is usually much more than you will make per print copy.

Non-fiction books generally sell for a slightly higher price point than fiction as readers are paying for information and an answer to a specific problem. Non-fiction readers expect the book to be helpful to them long term.

Another great idea is if you have more than one book, to price them differently. Have a short work of fiction like novellas, priced between $.99 to $2.99 and then longer books between $4.99 to $5.99. It's a great way to spread out your risk.

You can also bundle books together to create value packs at higher prices. If you have three ebooks in a series, which are normally priced at $4.99 or higher, you could bundle them together as a three ebook series for $9.99. This encourages readers to buy.

Consider pricing your book for free for a limited time. It's a great strategy to get more readers. Putting your book up for free on digital retailers like Amazon, will still bring you the most number of downloads. If you put your first book in a series for free, you'll also bring up your ranking in the Amazon algorithms.

Some authors have put the first book in a series on

perma-free(permanently free) which brings in new readers all the time.

A benefit of having your book for free is that your book appears on Amazon in the 'Also Bought' lists, which exposes your book and you as the author to more readers.

A quick way to get your book priced at permanently free, is by changing the price on Kobo and after that's done, contact Amazon to ask if they will price match.

If you want to learn more about pricing tips and strategies, read David Gaughran's helpful book *Let's Get Visible*.

Something To Try...

You're getting closer to the finish line. How exciting!

Your next step is to double check in Scrivener that you are using the novel template for your manuscript. If not, just go to File > New Project and click on Novel. Then copy and paste your manuscript with the appropriate chapters in that template.

Then go back to File > Compile and start the compiling process. At this point you might want to double check that you have a page at the back of your book that provides an incentive for readers to sign up for your newsletter and email list to receive a free book.

By doing this you'll start to add more readers to your

email list and they will benefit because they'll hear of new releases from you. It's win, win!

Also if you want to have a print book made, write your back cover description and your author biography. Formatting for a print book, I have outsourced in the past but you can learn to do through youtube tutorials.

You can learn simple steps on how to take your manuscript and how to do you layout so your book's interior looks awesome and then you're ready to upload it to KDP Print or IngramSpark for a print-on-demand book.

Now that Vellum is available(for Mac Users or for PC users using MacInCloud), that's a great option to use to format your ebook and print books. Learn how to use Vellum in a video tutorial on my website here: https://www.createastoryyoulove.com/vellum/

Once you've complied your ebook into .mobi for Amazon and epub for the other digital retailers, than save your completed file. Check how the ebook turned out on your kindle reader.

Read through it thoroughly to see if there's errors that need to be fixed. If you find errors, go back and fix them.

When you're happy with your ebook, save in Scrivener and save a backup to Google drive or to dropbox also.

Chapter Eight

E diting and Revision

As a writer, it's super helpful to have another set of eyes on your work before you put your book out into the world.

You can do your own rewrites and edit out the parts you don't like or that don't seem to flow, but in the end you need someone else to read through each sentence.

You might be asking, why is this important? Mainly, because it's really hard to be objective about your own work.

It's tough to catch mistakes once your eyes have read over a sentence or a scene a few times. It's weird how this works really, but as you keep reading over and over a section in your book, you become blind to typos because your mind learns to fill them in.

However the truth about typos and other small errors is that you can find them in traditionally published books as well as self published books.

But, if you've decided to go the self-published route, you need to choose your own editor. There are some great editors with reasonable prices, at www.upwork.com or www.guru.com.

Details are important. As a writer, you need to fix as many mistakes as possible if you expect to win over your readers.

To look professional, you need to get editing done on your work. As you continue to write, you'll soon learn your own strengths and weaknesses and how much editing you need after your first draft is finished.

However, the important thing to remember is that a book shouldn't be published without someone else(*other than you*) reading it.

I'll mention the different types of editing you may need and I'll focus more on what is out there for you as a Indie(*self-published*) author.

I'll start with the most expensive and far-reaching type of editing and then move to the lightest and more affordable options.

Developmental Editing

A developmental editor will help you develop the flow of your story.

This applies also to your nonfiction book too. This is the type of editing that takes a little longer and asks more questions of your story.

I remember when I finished the first draft of my first novel, I worked with a developmental editor and she asked me many questions that dug deeper into the story like: *How clear are your character's growth arc and motivation?*

How understandable and clear is your plot? What's going on in the middle of the book that seems to disrupt the flow of the story?(*Sadly, I got asked that many times*).

I had the privilege(said tongue in cheek) of deleting quite a few scenes and I even made major changes to the direction of the story's ending.

Even though it seemed like I was chopping up all my hard work, when I finally made the changes she suggested, the flow of the story was much better.

Most indie authors won't ever work with a developmental editor, partly because they cost a lot more and partly because if you work closely with your beta readers or if you're part of a critique group you'll most likely be getting your own unique version of a developmental edit.

If your goal is to continue to write and publish as an indie author, you might not need to use this type of editing.

I learned quite a lot from putting my first book

through a developmental edit. There's so much I didn't know as a new author that helped me write a better story while going through this type of deep editing.

With that being said, I still would recommend a deeper editing, even if it's only for your first novel.

It will really help you learn how to write a story that flows and connects better with your readers.

Line Editing

A line editor helps you put the semicolons, commas and pronouns in the right place. It's all those details that many writers - like me - struggle to get right.

They will suggest things for you to change and then you need to work to change the parts they've recommended.

Don't make the changes blindly and just agree with absolutely everything your editor says.

However, if their input makes sense and especially if your editor's ideas make your sentences and overall flow of the story or book sound better, then do follow their advice.

The wonderful thing about line editing, at least in my experience, is that it helps writers understand sentence structure better.

When I was being redundant with my words, or I needed to rephrase something, my editor would say, "think about changing this" and she even gave me possible ideas of how to change it to make it better.

Being a new writer, this helped me understand the flow of sentence structure and ultimately each scene and big picture of the story better.

Hiring a line editor would be something that would be really helpful to you as you finish your book.

If this doesn't work in your budget, at the very least get a few friends who are good at the English language to read your manuscript and make suggestions.

Proofreading

Proofreading comes after you've done your developmental and line edits.

Once you feel confident that your work has been polished to the best of your ability with either the help of an editor or someone you trust, then you are ready to send your manuscript directly to your proofreader.

The proofreader's job is to catch mistakes. They are good at catching when you've left out a word, when you've misspelled a word or where you've forgotten a period or apostrophe.

If you don't want to use an actual proofreader, then at least ask someone you know who really understands the English language well.

If you are asking a family member or a friend, double check that they are okay with it because this is the type of reading and correcting that is actual work, not pleasure.

You don't want to have a bunch of people you know

resenting you because they see proofreading your work as an imposition.

A much safer bet all around is to hire a proofreader to catch all the mistakes.

Beta Readers

Beta Readers are people who act as first readers of your book.

Very often these are family, friends or people you've gotten to know quite well in online groups. This is something you can ask your family or friends to do for you, if they like your work.

I've asked my husband and our two daughters to be Beta Readers of my first books and have also read through the second in the series. They are my biggest cheerleaders and I love that.

If you have people like this in your life, it can be such a big help. You get to hear from them which parts of the story they liked and why.

This feedback is incredibly helpful as you begin rewrites because it helps you as the author to understand what's working and what's not.

Ask for their Honest Opinion

Sometimes I will read out loud a scene I'm unsure about to my husband or girls.

This not only helps with plot, character development but also with typos and awkward phrasing.

However I need to ask them to try their best to be as honest as possible.

I know they are being gentle with me and trying to be as nice as possible when they talk about my book and I appreciate it. But, I remind them that my growth and success as a writer depends on reliable feedback.

When I've asked for help from some friends online who are part of my writers group, they've been very helpful in giving tips and suggestions on how to make my story better.

However one thing that I found helpful, is to ask specific questions. I'll ask about what they thought about certain scenes, or what they thought of certain characters.

I ask their advice on how I could make the story better. I've discovered that the more specific the questions, the better and more helpful the feedback.

The Art of Listening Is Learned Here

The people you've asked to read your book, whether it's family or friends, have taken their valuable time to read your work, so it's important that you as the author take the time to listen to what they have to say.

The art of listening to feedback, whether it's positive or negative is something that you grow into as an author.

In order to improve as a writer, you need to be able

to look objectively at your story and listen to constructive criticism because you never know just how it might help you to make the story better.

Sometimes, your readers might even offer great ideas for a future book or series. That happened to me in the Facebook Writers Group that I'm a part of and now I have so many ideas that keep running through my imagination. I love that.

When your readers are engaged in your work, they will offer all kinds of ideas of what they'd love to see in your story. Their hopes and dreams for your story, are really big clues for how to make your book better.

Keep in mind that your beta readers are *readers*. So if they have certain hopes for the story, most likely they're not the only ones among your readership. If you make your beta readers happy first, the rest will follow.

One word of warning however. When you send your work to beta readers, you want opinions and feedback, but you can't let yourself be tossed in every direction by differing opinions.

Listen to what they have to say, but still stand firm as the creator of the book. If your instincts are telling you to do it a certain way and you're hearing many different takes on how to do a certain scene, follow your instincts.

A good rule of thumb is if there are three or four people who have something similar to say about a character, scene or chapter, you should listen to that.

If it's only one person who suggests a certain change,

out of a handful of other readers, you could just ignore that suggestion.

The last thing I wanted to mention about beta readers is to be appreciative of the time they took to sit down and read your book.

Most people are very busy, so just the fact that they offered to be early readers and offer feedback on your book, is a great reason to be thankful.

Respect their time and their affection for you and do something nice for them especially if they are going to be beta readers on an ongoing basis.

Some Final Thoughts on Editing

The goal of editing and rewriting your story is so that your reader loves your story or your book. You want readers to read your work in a state of "flow."

You want to do all that you can as the author, so those who read what you've written aren't jarred out of experiencing the story because of mistakes or something else.

When you make decisions with your editor or as your beta readers offer suggestions, make your decisions based on what best serves the story flow.

Some writers who have more of a traditional publishing perspective, might tell you that you need lots of editors to produce a good manuscript.

They might even suggest that you need all of them.

However for an indie author, that might be a bit too much, unless you have large budget.

Of course it makes sense for a large publisher, but for the average self-published author, that will cost too much and there's very few indie authors who will earn that money back.

Instead, as an indie author, you should get good editing, but don't worry about getting perfect editing.

More than likely a good line editor, self-editing and a few beta readers will make your book great.

Something to Try...

Here are some steps to take next.

Once you have your first draft written, begin by doing a read through of your entire manuscript.

Then either print out your manuscript(that's what I do for my self-edits) or you can work in your document on Word, Scrivener, Google Docs, or whatever you use.

Start with the big picture of the story. Ask yourself questions like: *How does the overall story flow? Is your plot clear and understandable? How clear is your character's growth arc and motivations?*

If you're writing non-fiction ask yourself: *Is my overall vision and message for this book clear and easy to understand? Does each chapter flow well, with each connecting point that makes sense?*

Once you have the big picture of your fiction or non-fiction book figured out, then you can begin to read through line by line.

If you are using Scrivener for your writing software and if you're writing on a Mac, you can have Scrivener read what you've written back to you.

All you need to do is go up to the top menu, choose Edit > Speech >Start Speaking. Then Scrivener will start reading back to you from wherever you've placed your cursor. It's pretty fun and it helps you sort out words that you added that you should change or delete.

After you've checked for misspelled words, typos, and weird sounding phrases you could pass your book along to beta readers.

When the beta readers finish their read through and you've changed what you want to change, the next step is to find a line editor or proofreader. If you need help finding one, check out the above websites for some reasonably priced help.

After you've worked through your manuscript with your editor, that's it.

Your manuscript should be good to go at this point. But, there are a few more details to take care of before you put your book into the world.

Please read the next few chapters to find out the next steps to take.

Chapter Nine

Publishing Options for eBooks and Print Books

The beautiful thing about being an indie author is you get to choose where you want to publish your books.

There's many different digital stores like Amazon, Kobo, Barnes & Noble(Nook) and Apple.

Smashwords and Draft2Digital are aggregators who take your book and distribute it to other stores for you. Recently, Draft2Digital bought out Smashwords so we'll keep watching to see what changes that means for authors.

My own thoughts around publishing, is to have your book everywhere you can. I'm a big believer in not relying on only one digital store for all your income potential for your books.

My mom used to say, *don't keep all your eggs in one basket.* That notion is especially true for books, for the simple reason that each reader has their own preference of where they like to buy their books.

However, that being said I think sometimes it can be of great benefit for a first time author to enrol their first one or two books in Amazon's Kindle Unlimited program.

You will gain readers quickly and you will be able to earn income from not only people buying your book, but from pages read on Kindle Unlimited.

In this global market, the opportunities to sell your book in many different countries are incredible, and will only continue to expand.

So let's talk about some of what the more popular online retailers for books has to offer authors.

This chapter won't cover all the details, simply because these platforms are always changing. To know more details you can go to each website or search for tutorials on Google.

Amazon

In my own experience and from what I've read from other successful indie authors, Amazon is still their first go-to.

This digital retailer has the largest buying audience by far... *at least right now.*

For that reason alone, Amazon should be the place

you upload your ebook if you're self-publishing. Some authors have chosen to publish only on Amazon. Even though you can start there, I encourage you to self-publish on as many platforms as you can.

However, as you write and self-publish more books it's a wise business decision to choose to not have all your eggs in one basket.

Different readers shop at different retailers and throwing a wide net doesn't really take a lot of extra effort.

However, Amazon also has a program called KDP Select. What this means is if you give Amazon 90 days of exclusive rights to sell your book. You must agree not to publish more than 10 percent of your book KDP Select anywhere else. That will give you two main benefits.

First, you'll be able to choose any five days during your KDP Select period to make your book free. Free is a big drawing card for book readers, and so this will get new eyes on your book.

Second, KDP Select will also give Amazon Prime members the option to borrow your book, and you'll get paid for those borrows. So if your book isn't in KDP Select, readers won't be able to borrow your book.

I've heard authors talk of the benefits of going with KDP Select and then others who would prefer to keep their books on all platforms because they are earning more profit by doing that than from going exclusively with KDP Select for 90 days. The best way to know for sure is to test it out for yourself and see what works for you.

It's fairly simple to publish your book on Amazon. You need an .epub file(*Scrivener as well as Vellum compiles this for you*), a cover image and a product description for your book.

It's a big digital store with millions of customers so it's totally worth it to self-publish your book on Amazon.

Kobo

Kobo is a great digital store and so helpful for indie authors.

They have a self-publishing team called *Kobo Writing Life* that is easy to access and they always offer help fast.

I love the fact that you can track your sales with a graph and it shows you how many countries your book has sold in. Besides that they have a podcast that features interviews with bestselling authors and they are super helpful to authors.

A few years ago, Walmart partnered with Kobo for the sale of audiobooks, ebooks and e-readers.

So now indie authors can have their books in Walmart's digital store, which is exciting. Walmart ebooks includes a library of over six million titles, which is wonderful news for authors.

Kobo is growing into a global powerhouse and it is a growing hub for authors and an amazing place to publish and sell your books all the same.

Apple

Some authors do really well on Apple's digital bookstore but so far, that hasn't been the case for me.

However, my next goal is to learn how to market my books better on the iBooks platform. Some indie authors like Liliana Hart, sell more books at iBooks than at Amazon.

Some helpful tips she mentioned were to have the first book in a series for free, so readers can get a taste of your writing.

You can also set-up a preorder of your book. You can even put your book up for pre-order a year in advance, which really helps to get the word out for your book. Also, unlike Amazon, your pre-orders don't count against your overall rank.

However, you need to prepare ahead. Have a production schedule, so you can set up your pre-order to let iBooks know you have a new release coming out in three months, or whatever your schedule is.

It's a great idea to get your book uploaded onto Apple Books.

. . .

Barnes & Noble

Barnes and Noble's marketplace is a retailer where I don't get a lot of sales... *yet.* I'm hoping to change that.

However, some indie authors do really well there, and I hope you do too.

At Barnes & Noble it's difficult to really gain traction with advertising because it doesn't have the big affiliate program that Amazon does. This makes advertisers less likely to send traffic there.

Right now, it seems like one of the best ways to reach your ebook readers is through advertising through BookBub. If you can get listed there, you will have a much better chance at getting more of your ebooks sold at Barnes and Noble.

I upload my ebook to Barnes and Noble through Draft2Digital, instead of publishing it directly to that digital retailer.

It saves me time, and that way I can write books faster.

Smashwords

Like I mentioned, Smashwords - like Draft2Digital - is an aggregator, which means they take your book and distribute it to other stores for you.

Since, Draft2Digital recently bought Smashwords most likely authors will continue to see upcoming changes to the platform.

Some of the stores where they will distribute your book are Barnes & Noble, Amazon, Kobo, Apple, Sony and many others.

I like to upload to Amazon and Kobo directly because aggregators are sometimes slow to respond, and will bulldoze you into using a generic call to action at the end of your book, rather than one that's specific to each platform.

It's much more empowering to have more control and better results when you get your book onto some of the bigger stores directly.

When I first uploaded the files to Smashwords, I was rejected for "Premium Distribution." I wanted it in Premium Distribution because when it's accepted in there, then your book is sent to other retailers outside of Smashwords itself.

It took me quite a few tries before I was able to get the formatting just right for them to accept it for Premium Distribution.

Mark Coker(the founder of Smashwords) has a book called, *Smashwords Style Guide* that you can get on Amazon for free, which will take you through the steps of formatting your book so you can get it on the Premium Distribution list.

Despite the hassle with getting your book uploaded on Smashwords, it really is useful for a few reasons.

First, this is another store where readers can buy your book and you can sell your book there.

Second, they are a great distributor to smaller stores like Sony and other places.

Third, they are one of the few places that can get your book priced for free in Barnes & Noble. And that's important for price matching.

Something I haven't tried is to set up pre-orders at Barnes & Noble, which Smashwords lets you do. It's something to consider.

Draft2Digital

Draft2Digital is a publishing distribution center.

It gives authors a single portal where you can publish your book directly to other retailers.

It's much easier to use than Smashwords, without the headache of trying many times to get the formatting figured out.

I really think it's a good idea for most authors to upload their books directly to retailers where you will be getting most of your revenue stream.

Use these aggregators for getting your book to much smaller stores. But, if you've decided you would like the simplest solution, using one distributor like Smashwords or Draft2Digital might make more sense for you.

If you are an author that wants more control, then formatting your ebook and uploading it directly onto retailers like Amazon and Kobo would be a good idea.

You could use aggregators as the distributor for the smaller stores.

If you want to manage everything from one account, then it might be better to upload your book onto Smashwords or Draft2Digital. It's quite easy to do and it doesn't cost a penny.

Publishing a Print Book

Publishing your book into print, is something that many authors want to do. I love to have a physical copy of the books I write.

However, when choosing to get your book published into print you need to know your reasons and have realistic expectations.

It takes a bit of time to format your manuscript to get it ready for print. If you can pay a professional formatter to get your book ready for print, that's definitely easier and looks great.

However, you can also do it yourself by following these detailed series of blog posts by Garret Robinson if you want to format your book for print book using Scrivener.

In recent months, I've switched to formatting my print books using Vellum. You can find links to both at the end of this chapter.

I know many indie authors, myself included, who like to have a print copy of their books to put on their shelves.

There are many other possible to self-publish a print

book. You could use your book as a promotion or like a business card, or just pass along to friends.

Or when you go to conferences you could hand out a bunch of your books. You never know who will be interested and want to buy your books.

The really exciting thing about print-on-demand publishing is that you no longer have to buy 5,000 to 10,000 copies of your books at one time and store them in boxes in your garage.

Print on Demand publishing means that you can order a single copy and your readers can order one. You can also change the interior of your book whenever you want to and republish it the same day if you find a typo or discover something else you want to change. This is awesome.

So I've described a couple of print options that are make sense possibilities for indie authors below.

KDP Print(formerly CreateSpace)

Amazon(as of this writing), has merged CreateSpace together with their new KDP print, making KDP the single place to publish and manage your digital and print books on Amazon.

I used CreateSpace for years and found it simple and easy to use. As I'm still new to KDP Print, I'm still in the process of figuring it out, but I'm sure it'll be my new go to for my paperback print books.

I've loved learning to format ebooks using Scrivener from Joseph Michael's *Learn Scrivener Fast* training course. As for size, I use either the 6" x 9" or the 5.5" x 8.5" size for my print books, but there are many sizes for you to choose from.

As you setup your print book details, you'll also be asked if you want glossy or matte book cover finish and if you want the interior on white or cream colored paper. I sort of prefer the matte finish with the cream colored paper.

Next, you upload your files (KDP print guides you each step of the way), then after you've chosen your options and have gone through the required proofing steps, you'll be able to put your book up for sale. Readers will be able to buy your print book on Amazon stores in many countries.

Amazon offers a MatchBook program that you can choose to be part of. That way the readers who buy your print book can get the e-book version of the same book at a discount.

Since you want happy readers who have a good experience with you and your books, it might be a good thing to try this(I've added a link to Kindle Matchbook at the end of this chapter).

The beautiful thing is, once the book is uploaded, you get to hold your book in your hands. It won't be in the bookstores, but you'll be in print all the same. And that's an incredible feeling.

. . .

IngramSpark

For indie authors who want their print book distributed to retailers, IngramSpark is a great print-on-demand option.

Their prices are higher than KDP print's, but their paperbacks look and feel more professional. Right now their prices are a little over $49 for the setup fee and then you need to add proof costs and if you need to change your print book, extra fees are added to that.

This is a great option if you want to have your print books distributed to digital retailers like Kobo, iBooks, Barnes and Noble and Google Play.

With IngramSpark you also have the option to print hardcover copies of your book. If you have fans that want hardcover copies of your books, this is something to consider.

If you want a hardcover copy of your book, the 6" x 9" print size looks great. However, with this print book I chose to go with the 5.5 x 8.5 inch paperback size. I like that size for most of my books.

You can find more of my paperback books at my website here: https://memorablefictionbooks.com/

But, the great thing is you have many options to choose from. You'll also be able to choose the type of binding you want.

A "Clothbound" book has removable dust jackets over cloth covers and a "Casebound" book is a hardback that has the book's cover applied directly to the hard binding.

If you decide to use IngramSpark to distribute your print books and you use the standard bookseller discount, a buyer could walk into a bookstore and order your book through the seller's IngramSpark catalogue system.

It might be a possibility to arrange for bookstores to order books for author signings or to have your title in stock as a "local author" this way.

For most indie authors, getting your books into print is great to do for yourself or for your family and friends.

But, for most self-published authors it's the ebook where they find the most readers and sales.

Something To Try...

Take a look at the different digital retailers above.

Choose what you want to do. If you like what Amazon's KDP Select program offers, then enrol your book there.

If not, then consider your options. Do you want to upload some of your books directly to digital retailers, or do you want to use an aggregator to deliver all your ebooks.

If you want to upload your ebook yourself, try the major retailers first, like Amazon and Kobo and have an aggregator like Smashwords or Draft2Digital deliver your book to all the other stores.

Choose if you want a print copy made of your book for yourself or family and friends. If you decide to go for it, then once you figure out whether to go with KDP print or IngramSpark, you can get started.

Chapter Ten

Set Up Your Author Business and other Details Before You Self-Publish

When you choose to be a self-published author, at the same time you also become a small business owner.

You are an Author Entrepreneur.

The thought of being an entrepreneur used to really intimidate me. I had a tough time thinking of myself as a business person. I'd never had my own business before and wasn't sure how to begin.

However, when I read Joanna Penn's book *How To Make A Living With Your Writing,* I had an epiphany on what it meant to be an Author Entrepreneur. Somehow, her words helped me to frame my thinking in a positive light.

"Entrepreneurs create value from ideas." Joanna Penn

When I thought of being an indie author through that lens, I realized that writers are the quintessential entrepreneurs.

We take our ideas, form words and turn them into value every day.

Writers do this through inspiring, entertaining or giving information to others. In return for what we are offering others, writers are rewarded with scalable income.

Which is incredible when you think about it. As an author, you create once and you can sell your book over and over again.

In fact, even if it took you a year or two to write your book, you only invest your time once, but that book can sell one copy, ten, a hundred or thousands of copies.

Your book can benefit you for years to come and those who inherit your book royalties for up to seventy years after you die. I still find it amazing that as a writer, you can create value from books that will add income to your bottom line for years.

In the beginning, your scalable income might be small, but as you write more books and reach more readers, your income will continue to increase.

So it comes down to shifting your mental game around how you see yourself and embracing the possibilities that are waiting for you as an indie author.

. . .

How Do You Set Up Your Author Business?

Many self-published authors choose to set up a checking account, credit card, and PayPal account in their author name.

It's a good idea to set things up properly, right from the start. I did that too, only I set my business up in partnership with my husband.

However, I'm happy we started with a separate identity, because it's much easier to track expenses and income from one central place. It also makes tax time a lot easier.

Also, because I live in Canada, before I published my first book, I set up our EIN number with the IRS. That way we wouldn't have to worry about 30% withholding tax, once my first book and other digital products began to sell.

If you are a non-US author, check out this helpful blogpost written by indie author Karen Inglis at https://selfpublishingadventures.com/tax/.

If you choose to use your name or have a separate business name, do that before you self-publish your book. It will save you the hassle of figuring out everything later on.

Do you need to have an ISBN for your book?

There are some rumors out there that you need to have an ISBN in order to sell your book or to get on the NY Times bestseller list.

It's not true.

You can sell your ebooks on digital retailer sites, without ever buying an ISBN.

They call Indie ebooks without ISBNs the invisible "Shadow Industry." 30% of all ebooks sales do not have an ISBN. They also reported that 37% of Amazon's overall top 10,000 selling ebooks did not have ISBNs.

In other words, many indie authors are choosing not to spend money on ISBNs for their ebooks and it seems like that number is growing every year.

Retailers have their own way of numbering the books that they publish and if you're printing through KDP print, they will give you an ISBN for free.

However, if you do incorporate or use a publisher name that you want to have on your books, you won't want to use KDP print's free ISBN.

To keep your publisher name on all your books, you'll want to purchase your own ISBNs.

So how do you go about getting an ISBN if you want one?

To start with, you need to establish your self-publishing business identity, including the name of your "publishing house" and the address and telephone number(s) you have chosen to use.

These will be listed as your contact information in *Books in Print*. Then fill out the application at http://www.isbn.org. ISBNs aren't cheap.

A set of 10 ISBNs is around $300 as of this writing, so if you are planning to write more books, get enough to last for the next five years or so.

I should mention here, for authors who live in Canada, you can get your ISBN's for free when you click this link: http://www.bac-lac.gc.ca/eng/services/isbn-canada/Pages/isbn-canada.aspx.

Remember, if you choose to use an ISBN for your books, you'll need a separate ISBN for each edition and format of the book you publish.

For example, if you are offering the same title in a hardcover, a paperback and an ebook, each of these editions would require a separate ISBN. This helps a bookstore or customer to order the correct edition of the book they want.

Along with the barcode, you can have your ISBN translated into a worldwide compatible bar code, which allows your book to be sold through bookstores, online or in stores, or by distributors. Barcode scanning is what retailers use to sell books and book-related products.

You can get the barcode in several different formats: a film that can be "stripped" directly into your book cover art, an electronic file that can be incorporated into your electronic art, or a hardcopy that you can paste onto artwork.

You can get barcodes directly online at www.isbn.org. Barcodes usually cost less than $100.

For a bigger list of companies that provide barcodes go to, https://www.myidentifiers.com/barcode/main.

Many times, the graphic designer who designs your book cover will create a barcode for you at minimal cost. That's what I did with my first book.

Once you've assigned an ISBN to a product, you need to file an "Advance Book Information" form (ABI) to submit to Bowker.

You can also register your book information online at BowkerLink Publisher Access System(http://www.bowkerlink.com).

You can use the website above to change information about your books or publishing company(like if your address changes, etc). They'll add your title to the database of record for the ISBN Agency.

As a publisher, you are eligible for a free listing in directories such as *Books in Print, Words on Cassette, The Software Encyclopedia, Bowker's Complete Video Director,* etc.

Let me just say that many indie authors who choose to use an ISBN, just go with the ISBN provided by the platform they're publishing on. Many indie authors do this with their ebooks because it doesn't really matter much with ebooks.

However, if you get your print book done with KDP print and you decide to use the free ISBN they give you, it does make a difference. It means that you can't go and publish that same book(hardcover, paperback) somewhere other than KDP print.

There might be instances where you'll want to offer paperbacks via both KDP print and Ingram-

Spark, and if you don't use your own ISBN, you can't do that.

So if you plan to publish your print book in many different places, you'll want to buy and use your own ISBNs. If not, don't worry about it.

How do I copyright my book?

As soon as you've written your book, copyright is automatically yours.

It's also provable when you upload and publish your book at online retailers.

If you want, you can register your book at the copyright office to give yourself some added evidence that the book is yours.

In the past couple years, there have been court cases involving copyright infringement.

It might be useful for you as an author to register your book with the copyright office. Check out this website for more information: https://www.copyright.gov/registration/

I hope some of the above ideas help get you started as you set up your author business.

Something To Try...

Begin by choosing if you want to register your author name or adopt a "publisher" name.

Next step, is to set up a separate business account for your author income and expenses. If you are a non-US author, it might help to read through this helpful article at https://kareninglis.wordpress.com/tax/.

After you have that set up, decide if you want to add an ISBN to your book. If you choose to add an ISBN to your book, check out the links above. If you get your own ISBN, you can get your barcode at Bowker Barcode or www.isbn.org. Or you can also get it from your graphic designer, in most cases.

Then you assign your ISBN to your book and submit your book information http://www.bowker link.com, or if you self-publish in Canada go here: https://www.bac-lac.gc.ca/eng/services/isbn-canada/Pages/isbn-canada.aspx

Once you have that done, you should be ready to upload your ebook to the digital retailers of your choice and get your book ready for print on KDP Print or IngramSpark.

Chapter Eleven

B uild Your Platform

There are people already waiting to read your book. You might not think so, but it's true.

With over seven billion people in the world, there will be a segment of the population who will want to read what you have to say.

But, before you can offer them anything, you must find them. And before you can do that, you must create a place where they can gather around you. If you never build that place, they'll never even know you're there.

This next section is about learning how to build your own author platform that you own.

It's time to begin building your platform and finding those people who will love what you write.

As you start to do this, you will begin to build a base of people - a community - with your readers and establish yourself as an author.

Different places to build your platform

So what exactly does it mean to have a platform?

Have you ever walked down the sidewalk and noticed someone playing and singing or saw someone speaking passionately on a topic they love with a crowd gathered around them?

A platform is like that. It's a place to 'stand' and talk to those who want to hear what you have to say.

Since you're a writer, your voice will be heard through the written word. It makes sense, that the larger your platform, the more people you can reach.

Online digital retailers are platforms. Most people go to these places like Amazon, Kobo, iBooks etc., to find and buy your books.

If you rank higher on the bookseller lists then many of the other authors, you will have a lot of exposure to more readers.

Your books aren't the only place where you have a platform. If you're on social media, people are also listening to your voice and what you have to say.

That's a platform.

There are some writers who have tons of Twitter or Facebook friends, and therefore, have a big platform. It's true that if you are engaged on the social media platforms, and actually use them, you will begin to connect personally and talk with many more like-minded people.

You can use social media to talk about your upcoming book or project or just to get to know people that connect with you in a more personal way.

It really helps to have guidance and support from other writers who are also writing and marketing their books.

I know I've learned so much by connecting with other writers on Facebook groups.

I'm in a closed Facebook Group for Indie authors called 20Booksto50K that I've really found super helpful. You can do a search on Facebook for 20Booksto50K and ask to join.

There's lot of great value for indie authors, especially when you have a problem where you're not sure of the answer.

It's incredibly helpful to be able to chat with other indie authors who have either been where you are or are dealing with a similar dilemma at the same time as you.

However, there are some other groups that are for specific genres or reader focused.

Whichever genre you write, search for the name in the search bar on Facebook, and most likely, you'll find a group that's already been created for writers of that genre. If you don't see it, you can be the first one to start it.

Something to consider, as you continue to write

books you can create your own Facebook(or a group on a different platform) group for readers like I've started for my fiction books. It's a great way to build great relationships with your most dedicated readers.

I love to hear readers thoughts on what they like to read and why they like to read those specific books. I also love to share what I'm learning as an indie author, which is partly why I wrote this book.

The most important part of building a platform is to reach as many people as you can, offer them good value, and grow amazing relationships with them.

You can reach out by giving your readers real value and by being nice to them(i.e. having book giveaways, contests and simply saying "thanks" when readers leave you a nice comment on a social media page).

Anywhere you can reach out and talk to people is a great way to connect and will also help your platform grow.

Digital retailers and social media are great, but what happens if any one of those platforms - or heaven forbid - all of those platforms suddenly disappear? Your sales will go down or disappear completely.

Even though it's important to connect and build relationships on social media, it is vital that you don't rely on social media or digital booksellers - platforms you don't own and can't control - to be the only place you grow your audience.

To build your assets on property someone else owns is a bad idea. We've seen in the past how quickly social media platforms can change. MySpace used to be a thriving place that many musicians did well on.

Now, many MySpace musicians have switched to Facebook, but who knows how long Facebook will be around? The people who used MySpace wouldn't have guessed they would be transitioning to another platform.

The moral of the story here is that building your platform only using social media or digital booksellers, is fickle. You don't own it, so you can't control it.

Build your platform where you can control it.

That's not to say you shouldn't use the other platforms out there like Twitter, Facebook and, of course, the digital retailers, but your biggest connection to your readers should, when all is said and done, be from your own website and email list.

When you build your own website - for instance using a wordpress.org website, you have a cushion against sudden changes.

If Twitter would suddenly go away, you would still have your email list and you could direct your audience to the next social network that you choose.

On your own self-hosted website, if something happened to booksellers and you couldn't sell your books there(which would be really bad news), you would still be able to sell your books on your own platform.

Blogging

When I first started blogging, I used *Blogger* which was free - it's similar to wordpress.com - before I moved to a self-hosted website using wordpress.org.

However, the problem is that if you use either the free version of Blogger or Wordpress and create your blog there, they make the rules.

They put limits on the software(or plugins)you can add to your website to help it to function better and they put limits on your content. You can't use an opt-in form to collect email addresses on a wordpress (*.com*) website like you can if you're using a self-hosted wordpress (*.org*) website.

If they decide they want to shut you down one day, you don't have a say in it. Without warning, all the blogposts that you've written can disappear without a trace.

That's one of the reasons why, on my self-hosted websites, I backup my content, just so I don't lose everything. I also use WordFence, which is a free plug-in to help keep good security in place to lessen the chance of getting my website hacked.

So all of that is to say, as an author, it will benefit you to have your own website with a place on your website for people to sign up for your e-mail list. But, that doesn't mean you shouldn't consider connecting with people on social media too.

If your own website is your primary place - your home place - to connect with readers, then using Twitter and Facebook(or whatever your favorite social media places are) should be a secondary platform for you.

The key is to use those social media platforms as a way to keep bringing people back to your website.

What has worked well for me, and something I encourage you to try, is to have a website - that is a WordPress blog hosted on your own hosting plan - that is also a place where you blog.

You can find my step-by-step video tutorial on how to setup your WordPress website here: https://www.createastoryyoulove.com/how-to-setup-a-self-hosted-wordpress-author-website-video-tutorial/

Right now I pay about $10 a month for the hosting fee, which is reasonable. If the idea of blogging weekly seems overwhelming right now, just write one post a month, just so people can find you and begin to connect with you.

If this seems confusing you can always have someone set it up for you for a small fee.

Once you have chosen your domain name(as an author, consider having one website that is in your author name), then you're ready to go.

This website will be your platform and you can begin reaching out to readers and directing them to your website.

How do readers sign-up to your mailing list once they are there? That's what we'll talk about next.

Steps to Set Up Your Email List

This isn't as scary as it seems. It is a little technical

to set up your own self hosted WordPress website, but here are the steps that I hope help you get your website up and running quickly.

First Step is to get your website set up. You need a place to put your e-mail signup form.

It's really great if you can put this on the upper right hand side of your website, just for the simple reason that this is where readers of blogs are likely to look first.

A website on your own site with your own hosting plan like I mention above, is ideal. That way you have the freedom to do what you want on your website.

Second step is to find an e-mail service provider. There are quite a few to choose from. I use MailerLite because it's reasonably priced and delivers broadcast emails regularly to my readers.

Also, they have good customer support, which I've used quite a lot in order to figure out how to set up my own email list. There are other email providers like iContact, Aweber, Constant Contact, MailChimp or SendFox, to name a few.

If you're concerned about the price, MailerLite will help you get started, by letting you grow your list up to 1,000 subscribers for free.

In the end, the most important detail that matters is that you continue to add people to your list and regularly send emails that are packed with value for your readers.

Third step is to create a sign-up form that lets people join your list. You can watch videos from your service provider, that's what I did. I found videos on MailerLite that explained how to do this and I did a Live Chat with them too.

It's as simple as a short code that you copy and paste onto your sidebar. Consider enticing people to sign-up by offering them something for free or offer them something that isn't available anywhere else.

The key is to really listen to your readers and what they want from you. Use your list to make your readers happy because for writers, happy readers is really the end goal.

Keeping your readers happy will be a game changer for your author business.

Fourth step is to create an automatic reply message so readers who sign-up for your list will get an email back immediately. This is sometimes called an autoresponder message. This step is important because you want to appreciate and thank people for signing up to your e-mail list and you want to use this autoresponder to deliver the free bonuses you've promised for their sign-up.

These emails should be spontaneous and casual. Like you're talking to a good friend. Then after they get your email, you can also schedule an automatic reply, which are sometimes called 'follow-up messages.'

Fifth step is to start giving that link out to readers. The most important place to do this is at the back of your book. Write a Call To Action that will encourage readers to look at other books you've written.

Think of your reader when you're writing your CTA(call to action). What would compel them to go to your website at that moment and sign up for your list?

Also double check that your CTA link is clickable. There aren't many people who will walk to a computer and type your URL into a web browser.

They want to get to the link as fast as possible, right from the ebook they're reading at that moment.

If you are writing your book with Scrivener, this is easy to do. Just highlight the text you want to link, go to Edit, click Add Link and type it in. Test the link to make sure it works and you're good to go.

Once you've gone through all the steps, you'll be able to sit back and watch your email list grow. It might start off slowly, but over time it will grow.

Remember, each person is another reader that likes what you're doing, that might have otherwise never found your books or been added to your email list.

Growing Your Email List

Having a way that readers can contact you directly develops trust and grows your audience.

The best way to do that is by putting an "Author's Note" page at the end of every book you publish, and include your email address there.

You can create a new email address that you only use for readers, and that way your private email address stays private. It's fairly simple to create a new email account using gmail.

To have some way that readers can reach out to you is so important. On the "Author's Note" page, you can write something about how happy you are to get email from readers and that you would love it if they would reply back to the email you sent them.

If some of your readers do reach out, those conversations are priceless. With how busy everyone is nowadays, the fact that someone would take the time to write you back is amazing.

Cherish those emails, because it's a confirmation that you're making a difference with your books.

When you begin to build relationships with your readers through email, it's good to remember a couple of things.

Respond to those emails to connect with your fans. They'll really appreciate it and will become loyal readers. Also, when you reply, respond to their questions and respect them. It doesn't have to be a long email. Four or five sentences is great.

It's also super important that you send regular emails to your readers, like a regular newsletter.

If you don't see yourself as the marketing type, that's even better, because you don't want your emails to sound like marketing hype. The best way to connect with your readers is just by being yourself.

Building a list is something you must do as an author if you want to really be effective.

The biggest reason to reach out to your readers through email is because you don't want someone else to suddenly take away your ability to talk to your readers.

Your platform is essential to your business as an author, you don't want to risk a major change causing you to lose contact with your readers.

We are all aware of how quickly the websites we are so familiar with can change, so it's best to have a website of your own, as well as an email address. Then you won't be worried about the possibility of losing that connection.

An email list also ensures that when you talk about the new titles you have available, people will listen.

You can ask them for reviews. You can let readers know when you're doing a book signing or when you're having a special discount on one or two books.

If you have a series, you can be confident that there are readers who are eagerly waiting for the next book. You want to be able to email them and tell them when it's available, because they are as eager to buy as you are to make sales.

A spammy way to email your readers is to use high-pressure salesmanship or to use boring and impersonal emails like those you read from major retail stores.

You want to write your emails in such a way that you engage your readers and they pay attention to every word you say.

If you really think about what it is that you like from other authors who send you emails, then figure out what it is about their emails that you like, and model(not copy) what they're doing.

Write engaging letters that people love to get in their inbox. The beautiful thing is, the reason they joined your list in the first place is because they were interested in your work. So you really don't need to be bashful about letting them know when you have a new book release.

Adding links in your newsletter *so they can buy the books they already want to buy from you*, just makes sense. They won't be upset with you if you tell them about your books, unless you're doing it in a *buy my book now* kind-of-way with every newsletter.

Your readers are expecting new books and other products from you. They just want to get to know you as a friend and every once in awhile buy what you have to offer.

Your readers want to bond with you as a person, not only as a writer. It's great if you can chat with your readers by sending out an email once a week. So give them some of yourself.

It's simple really. Treat others how you want to be treated.

How Do You Find Your Readers?

Bonding with your readers, takes time.

That might not be what you wanted to hear, but in my experience and from what I've learned from other successful authors, that's the short and long of it. The best way to find readers is to write more books and have CTAs on the back of your books.

Consider having one of your books free so that people can check out your writing style and then it will lead them to your website and to more of the books you have available.

The awesome thing about books is that writing words is free. You can write more books because there is no limit to your imagination. So be generous and give away something for free, there's always more where that came from.

Another idea to consider is to begin podcasting about your book by using Scribliotech. Or you can write new chapters in Wattpad and find new readers that way. You could also read your stories using your own YouTube channel. Lots of people love video.

There are many different ways to create free content online. Find the way that works with you and your ideas and give it a try. When you try the idea, just make sure you're passionate about it and only start what you can finish.

Of course, one of the best ways, that's been a proven method to grow your list of readers, is to be generous to them.

If you want readers that stick with you and keep buying what you write, do your best to give them what they're asking for and keep doing it over and over again.

It won't be long until they also tell their friends about you.

Something To Try...

Now that you understand the importance of having your own website and a place for readers to sign-up for your email list, it's time to begin to set that up.

Start by setting up your website - preferably a self-hosted website so you have the most control - then go through the steps listed above to start a place for readers to sign-up for your email list.

Some good pages to have in place is an *about page*, a *contact page* and a page where people can buy your book.

Then you can write a blogpost so readers can begin to connect with you. As you begin to reach out to readers, you'll find more people signing up to your list who really want to hear what you have to say.

Give something away for free as an incentive for people to sign up to your list.

Some giveaway ideas: a free video, a short fiction book, an infographic or something else that is related to your brand.

Once you've done that, you're ready to begin marketing your book.

Chapter Twelve

D efining Your Brand and Marketing with Social Media

Your brand is simply the clear impression people have of you and your books whenever or wherever they find you.

Whether you do this consciously or subconsciously, you still have a brand.

It's way better to decide ahead of time what you want your brand to be - what you stand for - than to just let it happen to you.

When you work hard to create a consistent and clear presence that people can see - one that you've chosen - you are giving readers and others a feel of who you are and what they can expect from you and your books.

Your brand creates a feeling in people. For instance, when you think of fun cartoons from a well-known company based in Anaheim, California, you usually get a happy feeling(at least I do).

I remember going to the Florida Adventure Park when I was fifteen years old with my brother and his friend, and it was colorful, magical and clean.

They were creating a happy, safe and fun family experience that inspired your imagination. As a visitor I came away from there with the feeling that we had created a fun and happy family memory.

I've looked at this parks history and realized that the experience I had there is one that is shared by many other people and didn't happen by accident. The D-Corporation has worked hard to create and enhance that impression for families who continue to visit their adventure park year after year.

Creating your brand is not so different for writers. For example, Barbary Freethy, a best-selling contemporary romance indie author has built a brand around feel-good, suspense, love stories with a small town feel. And it works.

Readers love it and are drawn into the small town charm.

Similarly, mega-selling Indie author Bella Andre - who now ranks consistently on a #1 spot on Amazon alongside other well known authors - her brand is about sensual, empowered stories, enveloped in heady romance.

Yet, she does many interviews on blogs and via video. By all impressions, she's very approachable no matter how many fans follow her. If you're a Bella Andre fan, doesn't that help you bond better with Bella and her books?

It's important to realize your brand. This is how your public views you. You have a Unique Selling Proposition(USP). So what is yours? What are you that nobody else is? What do you offer readers that nobody else can?

More than anything else you must remember one thing about your brand. It must be consistent and you must not waiver from it.

Bonding with your readers always takes time. For that reason, writing more books - the kind that resonates with you and with your readers - is always the best way to find readers and turn them into raving fans.

The fact that it takes time is not something that many authors want to hear, but it's the truth.

Writing books consistently, especially when you are first starting out, feels complicated and burdensome. I get it. I think that's why it took me awhile to get the second book finished in my Historical Romantic Suspense series, because I wasn't sure if I was up to repeating the process.

If you're a new author, the last thing you might want to hear after all your hard work of finishing your first novel, is that you need to do it all again.

However, if you want to write for a living, the more

books you write, the wider the net you cast for more readers. This means that it's more likely that even more of your ideal readers will find you.

So write more books, because with each new book you're reaching even more readers.

Remember to put a compelling call to action at the back of all your books so that readers sign up for your email list.

The Power of Word of Mouth

Word of mouth for an author is very important.

You want readers discussing your books and telling their friends. In fact, this is one of the biggest ways people find books they love to read.

They read your book and loved it, and so they recommended your book to their mom and friends too.

If you're an avid reader, think back to the last time you picked up a book to read based on a recommendation from someone you know. It probably wasn't that long ago.

I know for myself, I'd much rather read a book based on what a friend said, then pick up a book based on some advertisement somewhere.

To attract more readers who talk about your books, you need to simply write more books that are worth sharing. Then do that over and over again.

Most readers will only recommend books after they had an excellent experience when they read it.

It's not good enough that it was an interesting story.

Do your books make people think and are they inspired by them? Do they get thrilled, sad or excited when they read your books?

Readers want an emotional experience that moves them in some way. The best way to get better at showing emotion is to write more books and to keep practicing your craft. This is something I'm learning.

Then, which each book you write, you'll get better at transporting readers into the story, which in turn will cause readers to bond with your characters, so they feel like they are invested in what happens to them. When that happens, it's a beautiful thing.

To make it easy for readers to begin reading your books, it really helps to have the first book in a series free for a limited time frame or you could make it permanently free once you have enough books in a series or standalone books to make it worth your while.

When you have one book free, then chances are when Sally tells Susan that she should really read one of your books. More than likely, Susan will read it because it costs her nothing.

You've taken away any reason for new readers not to try your books.

Building Relationships via Social Networks

For authors, having a growing list of readers is a

great thing. But, to connect with more readers means building relationships.

Sometimes that can seem like a really difficult thing to do, especially because many writers are also introverts.

So I thought I'd talk about how to develop relationships via social networks so you can have tons of friends and grow your platform all at the same time.

What really helped me, when I first started out in what seemed like the scary social media world, was a change in perspective. As I met the friends online I just started talking about what I was passionate about.

I was reaching out to people, listening to them and trying to do what I could to help. I've loved being able to reach out to more people by encouraging them, by being helpful and sharing my own journey.

There are many places on social media to reach out to people. To my delight, I've been able to develop friendships with many other writers, all in different stages of their writing journey.

Connecting with other authors has been so inspiring as well as helpful for my own journey. I hope you will reach out to other writers in your niche too.

Listed below are a few different social media platforms that I've found helpful.

You might choose different ones, and that's great. Go with the platform that you enjoy the most and is most helpful to you.

. . .

Wattpad

Right now, Wattpad is considered the world's largest platform for discovering, reading and sharing stories. With 24 million users, the majority of who are readers - only 10% are authors - it's a great place to find more readers.

Some beginning authors, who have shared their stories on Wattpad, have even got book deals from it, like Beth Reekles, a 17 year old who got a three book deal offer from her Wattled success. Wattpad is a popular site for teens, but about 25% of those who use the site are from age 18-30.

So, if you write YA or New Adult, you should consider putting your stories there.

Wattpad is a great place to test-run your stories. There are no gatekeepers and readers are not so concerned about critiquing your grammar or typos. It's more about the story, the characters and the emotion.

It's helpful to get a lot of feedback in comments from readers who get super involved in the story. As you start sharing your stories on Wattpad, remember to include a call to action at the end of the chapters as well as in your bio.

Use the serialization to advertise your book at the end and you can also link to a sales page so readers can click through to buy your book if they can't wait to read the rest of your book.

It's a great place to put the first book in a series, especially if that book is available for free.

Consider using Wattpad for writing practice and for fun and you'll soon start to find more readers.

Goodreads

Goodreads is the world's largest site for readers and book recommendations, with over 20 million members who are passionate about books.

Goodreads is a social network with a news feed that members look at first. Every time someone takes an action on your book, it goes out on the newsfeed and that gets your book out there to readers.

There's a "To Read" button that captures reader's interest. This is the first step to getting a review, and ultimately, your goal is to get reviews as this is what fuels the discovery of your books.

If you're just starting out on Goodreads, you need to have a regular member account, which once you have a book can be turned into an author page.

However, it's really helpful to continue to use Goodreads as a reader. You should be a reader first and be an active part of the reader network there.

Don't just talk about your own books, but be part of the conversation about other books and talk with other readers about books you find interesting.

Create your Author Profile including your author photo, your blog feed, a bio and then add your books. If you have videos, you can also add those.

Goodreads is also a great place to do giveaways for

your books. It's free to list a giveaway for the author and the reader.

It's great when other readers add your book to their shelves and review it. In this way, you can also reach people who would never have heard of you otherwise.

Giveaways are only open to authors with a physical print book because of potential customer service issues with ebook giveaways.

Most of all, Goodreads is a place for readers. So have some fun and join the groups that talk about the books you love to read, and about what you love to write.

Twitter

I find Twitter simple to use. It's one of social networks I go to because it's so easy to use. It's a little like texting because your messages can only be 280 characters long.

However, that's also what makes twitter a great and simple tool to connect with people.

Here are some tips that might help you use twitter effectively as an author.

First, it's helpful to decide on your niche and stick with it. People will follow you if they are interested in your tweets.

If you stay on topic, you'll get followers who are interested in you, they will retweet you and you'll get more followers in the niche.

That's how you'll expand your network. If you don't

stay on topic, your followers will be a mixture of people who like one thing but not the other and you won't appeal to them all.

Second, one of the biggest tips I've learned from following other successful authors, is to tweet information regularly that's helpful to the people in your niche.

This is what people retweet, they don't retweet personal updates very often. Then as people keep retweeting that information, you'll begin to have new followers who are interested in what you are sharing. You will begin to grow followers faster when you have a high percentage of retweets.

Third, you can find new people to connect with in your niche through #hashtags. Words like #writechat or #amwriting. Also when you attribute posts to others it gets their attention and creates a better relationship and it also enables you to tweet links without being blocked by Twitter as a spammer.

On twitter, it's much easier to create relationships with other bloggers in your niche. After awhile of mutual tweeting, you'll help each other by tweeting links, and hopefully guest posting and interviews will grow organically from that.

I've interviewed people on my podcast as a result of getting to know them through Twitter.

Here are a couple of things that you shouldn't do on Twitter. Don't auto-DM(Direct Message) people when they follow you. It shows you're a newbie and people know it's not a personal message, so it seems pointless.

Many people will unfollow because of auto-DMs, especially if you're trying to promote a product. Also don't tweet your own books or other products all the time.

Give first to others and you will receive.

Facebook

Facebook, like other social media channels, is a place to hang out, make friends and genuinely connect with people.

Facebook, in my experience, is one of the most social places to hang out. People post photos of friends and family and they talk a lot about what's going on in their lives. It's a great place to get to know people better.

For writers, beyond your own personal profile, it's really helpful if you can create a page for your author business. It may start small, but as people get to know you, it will continue to grow.

That's what I do. I have my own personal profile for family and friends and then I have a separate page, an author business page, where I connect with people.

Please don't set up a page on Facebook that is specifically for your book. That's short sighted, as you would need another page when you publish your next book.

An important part of social media, and Facebook specifically, is to always direct people back to your own website and capture their email addresses.

Post links to your site content so you are driving the

traffic that connects with you, back to a place that you own.

Make the most of multimedia. People engage with images, videos, podcasts as well as text posts.

I've noticed when I post random and fun questions, those often get the most interaction. Also, if you share emotional or inspirational quotes or funny posts, you'll get a lot of shares. Remember, people are on Facebook to laugh, to share their lives and to have fun.

What I've found really helpful is to get involved in Facebook groups. I'm part of a Fiction Writers group and part of a few Facebook groups for the community of writers who have joined online courses on writing and self-publishing.

There are many Facebook groups to choose from. I'm also part of a Facebook group for indie writers too.

Many of these groups, you can ask to join. I've found these groups to be a great support for writers and a great place to ask questions, be encouraged and share what I'm learning. We can learn a lot from each other.

Facebook does change on a regular basis. However the biggest thing I've discovered even through all the changes in the past few years, is that the most mean-ingful connections are made by sharing with others and commenting on their posts.

That's organic growth at its best. In a similar way, that's how relationships grow in real life.

As you continue to talk to people and respond to their comments, new connections continue to build over time that grow into lasting relationships. And that's really what we all want, isn't it?

TikTok

TikTok is the newest kid on the block, as far as social media sites go(as of this writing in summer 2022). If you love doing short video reels then this is definitely the place you want to be.

I have author friends who have been seeing a lot of success when they post short seven to ten second long videos. They write a quote from their novel or a short captivating summary and they do it in video form with some music and it draws in new readers every single day.

I've tried creating short videos with my pen name, and I've had some success reaching new readers. I feel like right now, TikTok still has the ability to organically reach a large reading audience.

So go head, and give it a try! :)

Grow Your Connections with Pinterest, Instagram, and LinkedIn

I'll talk briefly about a few other places where you might consider connecting with potential readers.

Of course there are so many social media networks out there that it's difficult to choose. Twitter and Facebook, are quite popular, so that's why I mentioned them first.

If you are just starting out on social media, I would recommend just starting with two networks, so you don't get overwhelmed. You can always add more later.

What I've done is to have a profile on most of the common social media places where other writers and readers connect.

However I mostly use Twitter and Facebook, but I do check for comments and chat a little with people over at the other networks like Pinterest, LinkedIn and Instagram.

Pinterest

Pinterest has really grown on me. I love it that you can set up many different boards, each focusing on one specific topic.

So I created a few different boards like: great blogs for writers, books for writers, podcasts, indie author tips, ideas for new books, separate boards for each book, and many more.

It's also helpful when you're creating new characters to pin a picture of an actor they look similar to and post their description.

Pinterest for the most part, is based on sharing pictures and videos. It's a search engine and social media site combination that emphasizes images.

As I've learned, it's very addictive, and if you love

photography, this might be your new fun place to hang-
out. Many authors I know are using Pinterest to create
Boards of their research and images that have inspired
their books.

It's a great network to connect with readers or other
writers because you can follow each other and re-pin
any pictures that you like to your own wall. See, I told
you I'm addicted!

LinkedIn

LinkedIn is really a social network for professionals.
So if you have a business book or a non-fiction book that
solves a problem, LinkedIn would be a great place to
share that.

It has become the number one professional social
network. I've been happy to connect with many authors,
bloggers and editors on LinkedIn.

Also, when others post new information on social
media and writing, I've found many posts there very
helpful for my own learning process.

I've noticed that the LinkedIn groups are quite
active so that can help you in answering your questions.

If you are the manager of a group on LinkedIn, you
can directly email people, so it can be a great place to
build a community around a certain topic.

Instagram

I love Instagram but I don't remember to post there very often. I probably post about once a week there, just whenever I take pics of something interesting on my smartphone that I want to share.

Sometimes I've created quote graphics with an app from my iPhone that I also post on Instagram.

Usually it's some thought or quote that is inspiring me that day. I really need to learn a little more about Instagram.

I have author friends who post pictures of their upcoming book covers, which is a great way to use Instagram.

Also I've noticed that people who follow you, love to have an inside look at your life, via the pictures you post of yourself, your dog or whatever.

I've also learned that if you add hashtags under your picture, that people will find you and your post faster. I've found many other authors and bloggers this way, and it's also a great way to connect as you like their post and comment on what they have to say.

So those are the social media networks that I use and have found helpful, each one to varying degrees.

If you are just starting out with social media, consider only starting with two social media accounts.

Starting small will help take away the feeling of being overwhelmed as you begin.

Some tips to help you grow your social network...

1. *Be a real person.* Don't just put out information all the time. Add a photo of your cat or where you went hiking. People connect with people, not information.

2. *Remember social media is long term*. It takes awhile for people to feel like they know, like and trust you. You need to be consistent over time and put in the effort to build relationships.

3. *It's important to be generous*. Ideally, you should be tweeting other people's stuff 80% of the time and only 20% of your tweets should be about you and your stuff. Being a giver goes a long way.

4. *On social media it's important to be consistent with what you share, so people know if they want to follow your stream*. If you're consistent with the topics you share, then people who are interested in that will start to follow you. Also don't post only once every two months as people will unfollow if you're not consistent with posting.

5. *Reaching people everywhere in the world, means it's helpful to schedule sharing your*

content. To take advantage of all the people who would like to connect with you and read your book, it's really helpful to use a scheduler.

I use *Buffer*, but other great schedulers are *Hootsuite* or *SocialOomph* and others.

I usually schedule about 3 days ahead of time, so about 90% of what I post is scheduled and then I pop in everyday about twice a day to chat with people for a few minutes. I find that system works good and that way I can focus more consistently on writing.

Social Media is one of the best ways to connect with people in your niche. As you continue to connect with people and build relationships, it will lead to more opportunities.

I've interviewed people because I developed a relationship with them first on Twitter. I've also guest posted on writer's blogs that I've met on Facebook.

I've found that if you are friendly, share other people's posts or books and continue to develop that relationship, that you'll find more opportunities open up to you. So go ahead, don't be shy. Get to know more people out there.

But also remember, if you've decided to work toward earning a full-time income writing books, then most of your time needs to be spent writing your next book.

Schedule when you're going to use Social Media, because if you don't schedule it, suddenly you've spent an hour on Facebook and you don't know where the time went.

What I've found helpful, is to set a count down timer(*I use one on Google*). I set it for 25 minutes and do timed writing during that time and then I take a little break and come back and do it all over again.

I hope that helps get you started with Social Media.

Something to try...

Begin by defining your brand. Ask yourself these questions: What are you that nobody else is? What do you offer readers that nobody else can?

Write down your answers. Once you have a better idea of what you offer people go to the next step.

Choose which social media platforms you would like to be on. If you're not sure, start with one or two you are most comfortable using. You don't want to get overwhelmed, so don't try to be on every platform.

Create your profile on those platforms, add a good photo and write in the biography section what you offer to people. Make it fun and interesting.

Then just start connecting with people who have similar interests to you. It's that simple.

When your book is finished, you can start mentioning interesting tidbits about your book.

Be creative when you share about your book. Try

sharing character quotes or unique pictures of the setting of your book. Readers will find that interesting.

Double check that you only mention your book 20% of the time. The other 80% should be about offering value to people that connect with you.

Do this and you'll begin reaching a lot of people who will love to connect and chat with you.

Chapter Thirteen

You've Published Your First Book. Now What?

You've published and marketed your first book.

Maybe you've even made a few sales. You've started connecting with people and potential readers through your website and social media.

Give yourself a pat on the back and a day to party!

You've done what most people only dream of doing, but never actually get around to doing.

Now what?

Now it's time to write the next book.

Right now you might be thinking there is no way you can do this again. If you are feeling overwhelmed at the thought of doing this all over again, I get it.

That's how I felt after my first novel was finally

published. I felt like I had poured my heart and soul into writing and came to *the end,* feeling empty.

You might be asking yourself, how will I write another book, when it was so hard to write the first one?

First, remember the feeling you just experienced of seeing your book on digital retail platforms and holding your very own print book in your hands for the first time. It's a new kind of euphoria isn't it?

Imagine how great it's going to feel to write and publish another book that you're passionate about.

Keep those good feelings tucked nearby in your memory box and pull them out whenever you need inspiration.

Then take a moment to *breathe.*

Let go of stress and pressure and really think about the next fiction story or non-fiction book you dream of writing.

I've learned that once I really understand my passion - my reason why - for writing the book, the thoughts come naturally and I get into the flow.

Try it for yourself. You might surprise yourself with how easily the words come to you.

I've heard many successful authors say that writing gets a little bit easier with each book. This, my second book - and a non-fiction book - it has been somewhat easier to write then my first novel.

The beautiful thing is, that when you realize that it will get easier at some point, it gives you the courage you need to write another book.

Before you know it, you'll be a seasoned pro.

Then you can start really thinking about what you want your long-term career as a writer to look like.

Consider making a Five Year Plan for what books you'd like to write and how you'd like to grow your author brand.

This is something I learned from bestselling indie author Denise Grover Swank.

You can listen to Denise's tips on creating a business plan in this podcast interview: https://www.createasto ryyoulove.com/denisegroverswank

If you have a plan of what you want to accomplish and a flexible production schedule to go with it, then you're more likely to hit the target you're aiming for.

I have a blank calendar that I printed off(from printable calendars) and I keep that above my writing desk.

I write my goals of when I want to be finished writing and editing a project. Of course, sometimes life gets in the way, but then I just reschedule.

Here's something else I've learned. The best marketing is to write and publish another book.

Learning to get better at the writing craft and to experiment with different genres, which writers love to do anyway, is really the secret to gaining momentum and building a life long career as a writer.

Making space in your life for creativity is so key.

Protect it, grow it and sometimes coddle it, and you'll be surprised by how you'll gain momentum as an author.

. . .

Writing Long Term

As your author business grows, you need to be able to manage what you've created, and even more importantly make time to grow your writing skills.

Your biggest asset as a writer is your ability to write. So you need to be able to do that in a way that is sustainable for you.

I'm realizing this more and more, as I learn to schedule time to write among all the other commitments that still need to happen everyday.

I'm learning how to take time to foster my creativity and to encourage other writers to do the same. It's a challenge, but I love doing this. I wouldn't trade this job for anything else.

The beautiful thing about being an indie author is that there is so much freedom.

You can keep trying new things and exploring what works and what doesn't. You don't have to stick with one type of book. You can write in many different genres or write as many different non-fiction books you feel compelled to write.

I have so many ideas still for books I want to write. For example, I want to write a stand alone series of western romances, a dystopian trilogy and a series of contemporary romance books(set on an island).

Some more novels I want to write are a sweet romance series based on fairytale retellings and small town cowboy romances(*I've written eight sweet and clean romances so far under a pen name*).

I've also started writing the first book in a series of seven middle grade fiction books about a young girl growing up in a farming community in the far North during the 1970s. *This series is inspired by true events from my childhood.*

So you can see, my ideas are varied but these are all book ideas I want to write about.

I love the freedom of this writing journey. Sure, it's a busy life and there's a ton to learn, but it's such an amazing adventure.

So keep being bold and brave.

I hope you continue to make room for creativity and write the stories you love.

Share your amazing books with the world... you'll be so glad you did.

ARE YOU READY TO BEGIN WRITING YOUR BOOK?

Join our mailing list and grab your FREE PDF Download: *7 Steps to Nail Down Your Novel Before You Start Writing!*
Go here: **https://www.createastoryyoulove. com/storytelling-made-simple-free-pdf/**

Lorna Faith

Books by Lorna Faith

The Storyteller's Roadmap Series For Writers

Book 1: *Write and Publish Your First Book*

Book 2: *Finish Your Book*

Book 3: *Pre-Order Storytelling Made Simple*(Only available at my New Shopify Author Website) here: **www.memorablefictionbooks.com.**

Historical Sweet Romance Series

Book 1: *Answering Annaveta*

Book 2: *Anchoring Annaveta*

Book 3: I need to wait a little while longer before I write the last book in this series. *But it's coming...*

Sweet Bumbleberry Island Sweet Romance Series

Dreaming of Love

Grab your FREE Historical Sweet Romance! Go here: www.lornafaith.com/free-book.

What I'm currently writing(as of summer/fall 2022)...

Book #1 in a 7 book Middle Grade Fiction series inspired by the true story of — our family of 13 people — as we pioneered land in the 1960s and 1970s.

A large family struggles to survive the wilderness of Canada's North to finally forge a clear path in the land and in the new community to make a place to call home.

Browse books by Lorna Faith and her pen name Melody Archer and get a discount*(use code: MFB10)* when you buy Direct from my Author Website here: https://memorablefictionbooks.com/

About the Author

Lorna Faith is an author of historical romance and nostalgic middle grade fiction she has in different stages of writing.

Currently, she is enjoying writing a new middle grade fiction series, inspired by her childhood and her large family as they pioneered land in the Canadian North. :)

Lorna has a growing website, focused on helping writers to get their books into the world.

Check out this Video and Blogpost series: *7 Steps to Nail Down Your Story Idea Before You Begin Writing*. **Read or Listen here:**

https://www.createastoryyoulove.com/part-1-brain-storm-story-ideas

Lorna's website for writers is dedicated to helping first-time writers, to write, self-publish and market their books.

Through many blogposts, podcasts and videos, Lorna shares what she has learned and continues to learn in hopes that it will help others to write the stories they love.

Besides enjoying adventures with her husband and four young adults, she dreams of travelling someday and soaking up even more historical inspiration, amazing architecture and exotic foods.

Lorna's happy place is writing more stories and helping writers get their stories into the world!

Connect with Lorna when you click on your favorite social media links below!

www.facebook.com/createastoryyoulove
www.instagram.com/createastoryyoulove
www.pinterest.ca/createastoryyou
www.youtube.com/c/CreateAStoryYouLove